# LEARNING TO BE WHITE

Thandeka

# LEARNING TO BE WHITE

## Money, Race, and God in America

**CONTINUUM**
New York • London

*For Jack C. Verheyden,*
*who showed me the infinite in the finite*

2002

The Continuum Publishing Group Inc
370 Lexington Avenue, New York, NY 10017

The Continuum Publishing Group Ltd
The Tower Building, 11 York Road, London SE1 7NX

Printed in the United States of America

**Library of Congress Cataloging-in-Publication Data**
Thandeka, 1946–
    Learning to be white : money, race, and God in America / Thandeka.
      p.    cm.
    Includes bibliographical references and index.
    ISBN 0-8264-1054-5   ISBN 0-8264-1292-0 (pbk)
    1. European Americans – Race identity.   2. Whites – United States – Race identity.   3. Whites – United States – Psychology.   4. Middle class – United States – Social conditions.   5. Whites – United States – Religion.   6. United States – Race relations.    I. Title.
E184.E95T47   1999
305.8'034073 – dc21                    98–43688

# CONTENTS

# PREFACE

When I was five, my mother decided that my formal training in art should begin. She was a sculptor and believed that my childish play must give way to "serious" artistic projects. And so she covered the kitchen table with newspaper, placed a mound of wet red clay on it, and told me to get to work. I did so but soon grew frustrated and pushed the clay to the floor.

"What's wrong?" my mother asked as she picked up the clay and placed it back on the table.

"I want to make a lion," I said, "but I can't do it."

"You don't understand," my mother gently but firmly replied. "When you create, you let the material show you what it wants to become."

Not understanding what she meant but knowing that I'd get into trouble if I didn't do something, I began to play with the clay again, but this time without any particular thing in mind. Suddenly, before my astonished eyes, I saw part of the shape of a rabbit in the clay.

"Mom," I explained, "there's a rabbit in the clay."

"Help it to get out," she said, and I did.

I often thought of my first art lesson as I wrestled with the research material and interviews for this book. Try as I might, I couldn't make sense of my data. I wanted to write a book about whites and their thoughts about their race, but the material would not permit it.

After endless false starts and numerous drafts I finally gave up all my preconceived ideas about what I should write about race, racial identities, and racism in white America. And something amazing appeared. I saw that

- No one is born white in America.

- The first racial victim of the white community is its own child.

- Racist acts are sometimes not motivated by white racist sentiment but by feelings of personal shame.

I could now write my book. My task was to make sense of these counter-intuitive insights.

New discoveries create new images.

I see a fork in the road.

To my right is a well-trodden path. The vista includes books, workshops, committees and projects, special programs and work-place seminars about how to get along with "them" — that is, the blacks. I hear the murmuring roar: What are we to do with/about/for them? What do they want (now)? Why can't they take care of themselves?

To my left is the other well-trodden path. I look down that road and see stall after stall packed high with books and government reports. I hear weary voices trying to figure out new ways to show them (the whites) what they're doing wrong. How can we stop them from being racists? Why won't they give up some of their privileges? Why are they so rigid and uncaring about everyone except themselves?

I stand at the place where both roads meet. I look behind me and see new travelers journeying forth. These sojourners are America's children.

The image fades as I offer a prayer for us all.

"Let us walk together children."

THANDEKA
Meadville/Lombard Theological School
Chicago, Illinois

# ACKNOWLEDGMENTS

I could not have written this book without the support of a community of friends and colleagues. Dr. Holland L. Hendrix, president of Union Theological Seminary when I moved to New York City in 1996, awarded me visiting scholar status and office space for two years, so that I could complete the research for this project and write the book. His assistant, Sandra K. Jones, was instrumental in making the arrangements that turned the possibility of working at Union into a reality. I express gratitude to Holly and Sandra as well as to the Union faculty and staff who provided me with a supportive academic environment for this project.

Next, I must thank the Reverend Dr. John. A. Buehrens, president of the Unitarian Universalist Association, for the institutional support and personal attention given to me as I worked through the various stages of this project. As a minister and theologian in this religious association, I found encouragement both in the theological conversations with John about the spiritual dimensions and practical implications of my project and in his keen interest in developing program formats for my work. I also thank Peggy Potter Smith, the president's administrative assistant, for her steady support in making my extended meetings with John possible.

Two friends and colleagues spent innumerable hours reading, critiquing, and editing various drafts of the chapters of this book: Kenneth Morrison, professor of religious studies at Arizona State University, and David Reich, editor of the *World* magazine of the Unitarian Universalist Association. Kenneth, a scholar in American history and religious studies whom I first met when he was a member of the faculty in UCLA's history department and I was a graduate student there, has been a friend for almost twenty years. The scholarly strength of the three historical chapters of this book is due, in no small measure, to Kenneth's steady critiques of my work and his running commentary about the requirements for an adequate historical account. I expanded the historical portion of this book from one chapter to three because of Kenneth's keen critiques of historical content and scholarly adequacy. His advice and editorial eye greatly strengthened the entire final manuscript.

Would that every scholar had David Reich as a friend and critic. David was unsparing with his editor's pencil, spending countless hours working through numerous versions of each chapter. I knew all along that I wanted to write this book for the general public as well as for academics, and I thought that my background as a professional journalist would make this task easy. Only after working with David's critiques and subtle alterations of my style did I begin to realize how difficult it would be. David, a fiction writer, essayist, and master editor, has been my writing teacher in this project.

Three other friends who carefully read early versions of my work and helped me think through the arguments and strategies for the project are Noreen Dean Dresser, Phyllis Cutler, and Claudia Hill. Without their detailed attention, support, and encouragement during the first stages of the writing project, this book could not have found its voice.

Frank Oveis, my editor at Continuum, was a firm critic, supportive spirit, and patient friend as I labored long in the field while deadlines came and went. Without his original belief in the promise of this project and his unflinching editorial advice and insight, my manuscript would not have been transformed into this book.

I am also deeply grateful for the support and insights of my agent, Edite Kroll, whose good humor, unflinching faith in me and my project, and steadfast push to finish the work helped bring this project to a timely end.

Janna Malamud Smith introduced me to the post-Freudian world of psychoanalytic shame theory. Claude Barbre and Michael Flynn were my conversation partners as I developed my theory about the feelings of shame often associated with the formation of a white racial identity. I am grateful to these three psychoanalytic theorists for their assistance.

Finally, I would like to thank Jesús Salvador Treviño, Bobbi Murray, and Carol Bandini, whose support enabled me to dedicate two years of my life to this project, and Dolores S. Williams, Catherine Keller, Jason Starr, Phyllis Trible, Kathleen T. Talvacchia, and David L. McDonagh — Manhattan friends who turned my two years in New York City into a movable feast.

# ONE

# WHITE

This is a book about race, money, and God. It begins with personal accounts of the ways in which Euro-Americans become white, then describes the economic predicament this has left them in, and ends where the recollections began — with dark revelations of feelings before memory and beyond white.

As an account of the process of becoming white, this book is filled with personal memories by Euro-Americans of small, seemingly inconsequential, defeats. Each defeat, however, when acknowledged, produces the disconcerting feeling that something about one's own white identity is not quite right. This sense of misalignment with one's own identity could serve as a definition of shame. And that is the place where our story begins.

## Dan

In college during the late 1950s, Dan joined a fraternity. With his prompting, his local chapter pledged a black student. When the chapter's national headquarters learned of this first step toward integration of its ranks, headquarters threatened to rescind the local chapter's charter unless the black student was expelled. The local chapter caved in to the pressure, and Dan was elected to tell the black student member he would have to leave the fraternity. Dan did it. "I felt so ashamed of what I did," he told me, and he began to cry. "I have carried this burden for forty years," he said. "I will carry it to my grave."

## Sarah

At age sixteen, Sarah brought her best friend home with her from high school. After the friend left, Sarah's mother told her not to in-

vite her friend home again. "Why?" Sarah asked, astonished and
confused. "Because she's colored," her mother responded. "That was
not an answer," Sarah thought to herself. It was obvious that her
friend was colored, but what kind of reason was that for not inviting
her to Sarah's house? So Sarah persisted, insisting that her mother
tell her the *real* reason for her action. None was forthcoming. The
indignant look on her mother's face, however, made Sarah realize
that if she persisted, she would jeopardize her mother's affection toward her. This awareness startled Sarah because she and her mother
were the best of friends. *Nothing* — Sarah had always believed until
that moment — could jeopardize their closeness. But now, she had
glimpsed the unimaginable, the unspeakable — the unthinkable. Her
relationship with her mother was not absolutely secure. It could
crumble. Horrified by what she had just glimpsed, Sarah severed
her friendship with the girl. But the damage had already been done.
Sarah's mother was no longer her best friend because Sarah now
knew she could no longer count on her mother's absolute allegiance.
Her mother's affection was conditional. It could be lost. After Sarah
recounted her story to me, she said she had not thought of this incident in twenty years. She also said that until now, she had never
consciously said to herself that for her the deepest tragedy in this
incident was *her loss of trust in her mother's love.* Sarah, like Dan,
began to cry.

The feelings both Dan and Sarah had cast off years ago in order
to remain members in good standing in their communities had come
back. The sentiments that had originally gotten them into trouble
with members of their own racial group had returned. The recollections of early experiences of the discovery that their behavior
must be governed by white racial rules of conduct produced tears.
Why? Shame.

This answer did not come easily to mind. I first had to discover
the question, which meant making sense of a series of incidents I
could not explain using any of the racial terms I had long employed
when confronting white racial intransigence. I readily used words
like *racism, prejudice,* and *supremacy* to both explain and judge the
patterns of white behavior that continually displayed themselves before my mind's eye. But in 1991, I was confronted with an experience
that would not let itself be reduced to racial terms.

I had recently moved to a Massachusetts hamlet to teach at a local
college. Several weeks after arriving on campus, I had lunch with a

member of the college staff. My luncheon partner, a fifth generation Smith College graduate with a New England genealogy older than the state and a portfolio perhaps as wealthy, wanting to get to know me, asked what it felt like to be black.

I was not offended by her query. Her face was open; her eyes were friendly and engaged. She simply believed that *nothing* from her own background or experience could help her understand me. I knew better. I had been assigned a race by America's pervasive socialization process, and so had she. I thus believed that if she drew upon her own experience of being "raced," she might then be able to see what we had in common. But how could I make her *conscious* of the racialization process to which her own Euro-American community had subjected her? Searching for an answer to this question, I invented the Race Game and invited her to play it for a week.

The Race Game, as my luncheon partner very quickly discovered, had only one rule. For the next seven days, she must use the ascriptive term *white* whenever she mentioned the name of one of her Euro-American cohorts. She must say, for instance, "my white husband, Phil," or "my white friend Julie," or "my lovely white child Jackie." ... I guaranteed her that if she did this for a week and then met me for lunch, I could answer her question using terms she would understand. We never had lunch together again. Apparently my suggestion had made her uncomfortable.

African Americans have learned to use a racial language to describe themselves and others. Euro-Americans also have learned a pervasive racial language. But in their racial lexicon, their own racial group becomes the great unsaid.[1] I wanted my luncheon partner to give voice to her whiteness as the racial unsaid in her life. By consciously referring to this unvoiced color, she would become aware of what it feels like to take on and maintain a racial identity in America. Or so I thought.

Later in the semester, I recounted this unresolved lunchtime saga to a faculty colleague, who immediately blushed and then responded preemptively, saying, "Don't ask me to do that; I'm about to go on sabbatical." Why was the very prospect of playing the Race Game so daunting? Perplexed, I decided to describe these two responses to my Race Game during my next public lecture and then invite the audience to collectively reflect upon them. During the course of this public discussion, one woman challenged all of the other Euro-

Americans present to play the Race Game for the rest of the day and then report back to me by mail. Enthusiasm ran high.

A month later, I received my one and only letter from these enthusiasts — sent by the Euro-American woman who had originally proffered the challenge. She could not do it, she wrote apologetically, though she hoped someday to have the courage to do so. Courage? Why courage? What had I asked her to endure? What was she afraid of seeing? What didn't she want to feel? To glimpse? To know?

To answer these questions, I began a series of workshops with Euro-Americans in various parts of the country. I used church settings and regional and national meetings as venues for my project. Any occasion at which a number of Euro-Americans gathered to hear me speak became an opportunity. I conducted workshops at such national forums as the Common Boundary, an annual conference devoted to spiritual exploration and personal psychological development, and held public conversations on the topic at the first national Summit on Ethics and Meaning sponsored by the Foundation on Ethics and Meaning and *Tikkun* magazine. I asked Euro-American colleagues to tell me their stories and turned to strangers at dinner parties to learn their racial tales.

Of course, since my interlocutors weren't randomly selected, the accounts I shall present do not constitute a social-scientific survey, nor is this study a work of social science. I am a theologian interested in the way that issues of racial self-identity merge with religious sentiment and determine social behavior. I thus saw my interviews as a chance to enter into conversation with Euro-Americans who are not self-defined racists so that I could understand why it is so difficult for them to describe themselves and other Euro-Americans in racial terms. They do not hesitate, as I've pointed out, to make racial references to others, but they avoid making racial references to themselves and their own community, a gap in racial ascriptions demonstrated by my luncheon partner, who could easily refer to me as "black" but could not refer to herself and her companions as "white." So, too, was this gap revealed by the Euro-American woman who confessed her lack of courage to play the Race Game with other Euro-Americans. I wanted to know what feelings lay behind the word *white* that were too potent to be faced.

I began my queries simply. I asked Euro-Americans about their earliest memory of incidents that helped form their white racial identities. I conducted workshops to this end: to listen to Euro-American adults recount early memories of forming a racial identity. As a Unitarian Universalist minister, my venue was often but not always meetings of this liberal religious association with roots deep in Puritan America, New England traditions, Protestant ethic sentiment, and Congregational and Baptist histories.

In the remainder of this chapter, I present a sampling of these personal recollections, whose similarities cut across differences in religious affiliation, class background, and age. These accounts progress from simple to more complex as the persons I talked with reflect more deeply upon the feelings they had to put aside in order to remain a member in good standing of their own communities. As the reflections become more complex, the individuals' sense of moral failure and loss of self-respect deepens.

## Frank

Frank[2] remembers putting a coin in his mouth when he was five. His mother disgustedly told him not to put coins in his mouth because "niggers keep them in their underwear." Frank said he felt both confused and wrong. He knew that he would have to be more careful about what he did in the future.

## Jack

When Jack was five, his parents gave him a birthday party and invited his relatives with their children. He remembers going to the gate of his backyard and calling his friends over to join them. His friends, black, entered the yard. Jack became aware of how uncomfortable his parents were with the presence of his friends among them. He knew he had somehow done something wrong and was sorry.

## Mike

Mike, at age four or five, was walking down the street with his father and uncle. They passed by an interracial couple. The man was black, the woman white. Mike's father and uncle began a series of critical statements about the man and descriptions of the kind of woman his companion must be. Mike remembers feeling uncertain and confused. He now knew that there was a certain way he must act when he grew up, but he was unsure what it was and whether he could do it.

## Jay

Jay's parents took him on a car tour of the black area in his city when he was four. His parents knew he had never seen black people before and did not want him to embarrass the family by staring at "them" when the family went to New York on vacation the following month. Jay, now an attorney, told this story to me during dinner at his sister's home. His sister Fran, a colleague who had invited me to dinner, expressed surprise as she listened to the story of her older brother's formal induction into whiteness by their parents. "You never told me they did that," Fran protested. Jay smiled weakly and shrugged as if to say, "What was there to tell?" Nothing more was said.

## Jackie

In high school, Jackie talked about one of her teachers so often as someone who was playing a formative role in her education that her parents encouraged her to invite him home for dinner. Jackie remembers her mother's flushed and astonished face when she opened the door and discovered that the teacher was black. After he left, Jackie's parents were outraged that she had not told them of his race, making Jackie feel she had done something wrong, that she had broken a rule that until that moment she did not realize existed. She was sorry she had embarrassed her parents and knew she must be careful not to embarrass them again in the future.

## Sally

Sally's parents, strong civil rights supporters, preached racial equality both at home and in the streets. Sally was thus flabbergasted when her parents prevented her from going out with a high school friend who came to pick her up for a Friday night date. He was black. The parents sent him away and forbade her to date him. "What will our neighbors say if they see you on the arms of a black man?" Sally was furious with them and thought them hypocrites. But she submitted to their dictates. "What was I going to do?" she asked rhetorically. "Rebel? Not in my household. They would have disowned me."

## Terry

Terry, who had grown up in a small New England town, never saw a black person until he went to college. In college, there were only a few black students in Terry's dorm, and they always sat together at the same table in the dining hall. Terry felt the urge to go over, say hello, and join them. But this would mean he would have to leave his own group of friends. Would he be allowed to return? He wasn't sure. Rather than risk rejection, for four years, Terry said, "I simply buried my head in my soup."

## Dan

Dan, a well-heeled Boston Presbyterian minister, grew up in a New England town in which only a few African Americans lived. Dan and I had worked on several interfaith committees together, and whenever I was in town, we would get together for lunch. He told me his early memories as we lunched together in a small, elegant restaurant near Beacon Hill. When he was very young, his father, who was an alcoholic, told Dan: "Black people are inferior." Dan did not believe him. His dad lied about many things, so why should he be right about this? Dan next remembered going to Washington in 1952 with his classmates for their eighth-grade graduation trip. En route, Dan saw "colored" and "white" signs posted on bathroom doors and hung on the walls behind the public drinking fountains. Never having been in the South before, Dan found these signs both odd and troubling. He believed, however, that he was the only one in his group who had noticed them and sensed that there was something terribly wrong, because no one said anything about the signs — not even his teacher. So he buried the troubled feelings that had been prompted by these signs. At age fourteen, Dan was certain only he knew that something was radically wrong. America's racial policies thus became his personal secret — or so he thought.

I was amazed by Dan's story. Segregation had never been a "personal secret" in my life, I said. I lived in Washington, D.C., and then Dallas in 1952 and at six already knew which stores my parents and I could enter and be treated decently. Whenever we went downtown, my father always prepared for the worst. He kept a small notebook in the inside pocket of his suit jacket. Whenever a salesclerk would not wait on us, my father would remove the notebook from his pocket, take out his fountain pen, walk up to the clerk, and say, "May I have your name, please?" This gesture usually filled the clerk with fear and sometimes brought the desired result: service.

Dan now elaborated on his earlier comments. He said that he came to realize that each sign indicated the benefits accrued to the whites. The facilities designated for this group were clearly superior in comfort, upkeep, and convenience to those for the coloreds. The signs clearly indicated that there was no middle ground of safety for the onlooker. Seeing them, Dan realized that one was either colored or white.

As Dan's recollections continued, he told me the story of the fraternity incident (recounted at the beginning of this chapter) in which he told his colored fraternity brother to leave their fraternity house. After telling that story, Dan began to cry.

The couple at the next table tried not to notice Dan's breakdown. The waiter avoided our table. As Dan regained his composure, I retained mine. I could see his pain. I felt empathy for his suffering but was troubled by his lack of courage. Dan's tears revealed the depth of the compromise he had made with himself rather than risk venturing beyond the socially mandated strictures of whiteness.

I realized that being white for Dan was not a matter of racist conviction but a matter of survival, not a privilege but a penalty: the pound of flesh exacted for the right to be excluded from the excluded. As Dan's tears revealed, the internal price exacted from him for his ongoing membership in the "white" race was psychic tension and discomfort.

To explain his distress as the emotional fallout from white prejudice or white racism would slight Dan's own experience of having been at acute risk of being cast beyond the pale of the "white" world and into the realm of the "colored." In going along with his fraternity, he stepped back from the brink of his social perdition. Dan had learned early on that one is either white or colored.

The nature of the agony brought on by his refusal to risk exile thus could not be grasped using the standard racial categories of judgment and damnation that assume discriminatory racial acts against others by Euro-Americans always arise from racism, prejudice, and bigotry.[3] Such an approach would simply racialize the deepest level of Dan's distress: his need to retain membership in his own community of caretakers and peers. The charge of racism would thus act like a prisoner's stun belt used to exact a confession. His tears would count as evidence of his sinfulness. Dan's internal turmoil, in a word, would become prima facie evidence of guilt. Although he is not a racist, Dan might confess his guilt as a racist because this was the only way to stop the charge of racism for his act and also because *racism* was the only category he had to express a deeper loss and regret: his stifled feelings and blunted desires for a more inclusive community. But Dan did not cry during our lunch together in the restaurant because he was a racist. He cried because his impulses to moral action had been slain by his own fear of racial exile.

Dan, in effect, was a wailer at the wake of his own moral standing. It was evident that his moral failure of nerve had brought on a loss of self-respect. But behind this moral failure was a more original fear: exile. Dan's ability to set aside his own resonant feelings and act against his own moral scruples was initially not his own doing but his undoing. It was the attempt of the child to muffle its own feelings so that it would not be exiled.

We have only to remember Dan's earlier silence as an eighth grader in the South looking at the colored and white signs. This silence reminded me of the ubiquitous fears and "collective feeling of vulnerability" of women who have an ancient, collective sense of being at risk. As therapist and educator Dana Crowley Jack notes in her book *Silencing the Self: Women and Depression,* many of her clients quite often forced themselves to stop thinking and judging their thoughts in order to silence their own voices and opinions. They muffled their feelings of anger and resentment and thus, in effect, "stifled themselves" in order to avoid the threat of annihilation, conceal their feelings of unlovability, or hide those feelings and perceptions that they believed, if revealed, would be judged "wrong."[4]

Dan, like these women, learned to stifle himself in the face of ancient, collective feelings of being vulnerable and at risk within one's own (racial) community. But unlike the silence of the women who sought Dana Crowley Jack's help, Dan's silence was received by the world as a nonevent. The nature of the silence required for the formation of his white identity had yet to be noted in the chronicles of our nation's psychic life. Rather, Dan's silence would be explained as racist sentiment or liberal insouciance. Yet neither explanation explained the distress revealed by Dan's tears.

Every Euro-American I asked could recount a process by means of which he or she began to think of himself or herself as white. Most of these accounts were initially recalled as *objectively* seamless events. A rupture with the primary group had not occurred. Still, there were striking differences between the stories. Jay's story and the silence surrounding his initiation into whiteness by his parents had a different texture from the silence that pervaded Dan's experiences. Behind Dan's silence lurked an aching defeat. Behind Jay's silence lay nothing. He had never told his sister about this event because he believed there was nothing to be said. Jay had simply learned something about the way things are: there are black people and "they" live/belong over there — beyond the pale. It was as if everyone else already knew this. Jay simply had to catch up. The protocol associated with this new knowledge was equally self-evident: don't stare at *them*. The deeper implications of the message Jay received would develop over time: don't even notice that they are there. Such behavior, of course, is described by Ralph Ellison's protagonist in *Invisible Man:* "I am invisible, understand, simply because people refuse to see me."

After listening to several hundred Euro-Americans recount their early recollections of experiences that not only made them think of themselves as white but also taught them to act in ways that would keep them within this racial pale, I learned to doubt the validity of other Euro-Americans' initial claims that there were no such childhood incidents in their own lives. Rather, I began to suspect that many of them had simply forgotten the incidents. My experience with Dorothy became typical of the kinds of encounters I now began to have with Euro-Americans who wanted to know something about the nature of my work but who could not think of themselves as "white."

## Dorothy

I met Dorothy, a middle-aged Euro-American woman, at a dinner party in an Upper West Side Manhattan apartment. We had been introduced by our host: Dorothy was a "poet," whose most recent volume of poetry was prominently displayed on the coffee table in front of the couch on which we were seated; I was a "writer" working on white identity issues. After our host departed, Dorothy wanted to know what a "white identity" was. She did not have one, she assured me. She was simply an American. I could help her find hers, I responded, if she wanted to know what it looked like. Her interest piqued, she accepted the offer. True to form, I asked her to recollect her earliest memory of knowing what it means to be white. After a little excavation, she finally found the memory. It was this: when Dorothy was five, she and her family lived in Mexico for a year. Although her family's housekeeper brought her daughter, who was also five, to work, Dorothy's parents forbade her to play with the little girl. Dorothy, in fact, was never allowed to play with any Mexican children, and she and her two brothers were forbidden to venture beyond the gates of their backyard. Dorothy remembered her feelings of sadness and regret. The Mexican children and their parents seemed so much more at ease with themselves and each other. They seemed warm and physically close, unlike her own family, whose manners and expressions were cold and constrained.

Dorothy told me she had not thought of these feelings in years. She confessed that she now recalled how often, during that year, she wished to be brown. I suggested that the term *white* might not mean anything consciously to her *today* because it had too much negative meaning for her when she was five. She agreed and now expressed surprise that she had not written about these feelings, memories, or experiences in her work. She said much of her life had been devoted to freeing herself from the emotional strictures imposed on her by her parents. Most of her poetry was about them and the way they had drained life out of her. She reiterated her astonishment that this set of memories had not surfaced in her work. As she blushed, the resurrected feelings of the child seemed to disappear.

"You know," Dorothy now said pointedly, "you are the first black I've ever felt comfortable with talking about racism."

I said, "Why is it so easy for you to think of me as a 'black,' and yet until a few minutes ago you could not make any sense out of thinking about yourself as a 'white'? Further, were we really talking about racism? And if so, whose? Your parents'? Yours? That of the five-year-old girl who wanted to be brown?"[5]

Dorothy was silent for a long moment. Her silence was self-conscious and thus made me think of Dan's considered silence in the bus and his silenced protest in his frat house.

"I now understand what I've just done, and I'm horrified," she confessed. Dorothy was horrified because she now realized that if I were a black, she, too, must have a race: the one that had enraged her as a child. Dorothy realized that she had indeed learned to think of others *and* herself in racial terms. Not surprisingly, Dorothy now confessed that she was afraid to say anything else — not because I might condemn her, she said, but much more tellingly because, as she put it, "I might not like what I hear myself saying." Her insights had outstripped her racial vocabulary. If she'd been forced to listen to herself continue to talk, she would have had to listen to a white woman speak in ways that the five-year-old child would have despised. She did not want to listen to such talk. Nor did I. Our conversation very quickly came to an end.

I eventually decided to use the term *white shame* to designate the complex of reactions called forth when Dorothy addressed her own contradictory racial statements, emotions, and mental states. I called the experience *shame* because it involved the discovery of an unresolved conflict within Dorothy that, when discovered, made her feel flawed. I called the experience *white* because of the racial context in which she had discovered her internal conflict.

Shame is an emotional display of a hidden civil war. It is a pitched battle by a self against itself in order to stop feeling what it is not supposed to feel: forbidden desires and prohibited feelings that render one different. Such desires and felt differences must be suppressed or blocked off in some way because one's community deems them to be bad.[6] The ensuing internal battle often ends as a stalemate, a momentary paralysis marked by the red flag of a blush or the cold sweat of a frozen grimace. Experiences of shame are self-exposures that lower one's own sense of personal esteem and respect. They are private snapshots of embarrassing features of the self. Looking at these uncomplimentary mug shots, one feels shame as in the feeling that "I am unlovable."[7] Such feelings actually result from the failure of the parents or caretakers to love the child adequately,[8] *but the child blames itself rather than its parent or caretaking environment.*

Guilt, by contrast with shame, is a feeling that results from a wrongful deed, a self-condemnation for what one has done.[9] A penalty can be exacted for this wrongful act. Recompense can be made and restitution paid. Not so with shame. Nothing can be done because shame results not from something one did wrong but rather from something wrong with oneself.

The experience of shame is thus a negative self-exposure, a revelation of forbidden desires. The self exposed is incongruous with itself.[10] It is seen as who it is not supposed to be. It feels what it is not supposed to feel. It is aware of what it is not supposed to know. This difference between these two incongruous states of the self is the difference between a forbidden body-based feeling (the biological aspect of an emotion: an affect) and the way it is thought about. The affect + the thought = the emotion called *shame*.[11]

As noted above, I decided to call Dorothy's experience *white* shame because her feelings of shame were discovered within the framework of an examination of what having a white racial identity meant to her. Her discomfort with the term *white* as a locus for her own racial identity seemed akin to the predicament of a woman in a *New Yorker* cartoon who, standing next to her husband in a living room filled with partygoers, says, "What do you mean 'let's go home?' We are home." Whiteness was not a comfort zone for Dorothy. White shame is this deeply private feeling of not being at home within one's own white community.

I developed the concept of white shame to refer to the pattern of feelings and behavior that I had begun to see emerge as I listened to various incidents recounted by other Euro-Americans and that was vividly displayed by Dorothy. The Euro-American child, I now believed, is a racial victim of its own white community of parents, caretakers, and peers, who attack it because it does not yet have a white racial identity. Rather than continue to suffer such attacks, the Euro-American child defends itself by creating a white racial identity for itself. It begins to think and act like its community's ideal of a white self. When the adult recalls the feelings and ideas it had to set aside in order to mount this defense, it feels shame. More precisely, white shame. Dorothy had recalled the feelings of the child whose parents wanted to love a *white* child. The parts of her that were not white had to be set aside as unloved and therefore unlovable.

## Douglas

Douglas, a doctoral candidate in theology at a seminary in Chicago, served on the lecture committee that invited me to speak on campus in January 1997. As was my habit, at the end of my formal presentation, I invited the Euro-Americans in the audience to play the Race Game and then call me with the results. The Race Game, I told them, has only one rule. For a week, the player, in all white settings, must use the word *white* whenever he or she mentions the name of a Euro-American. A week after the lecture, Douglas called. He had played the game.

When I returned to Chicago in March, we met and went for a walk in Hyde Park. I had not wanted to know the details of his experience until I was in his presence. I wanted to look at his face and observe his gestures and body language as he described his experience. I wanted to see what could not be said. A blush, for example. I did not interrupt Douglas as he recounted his experience of playing the Race Game for a week:

> Every time I decided to play the game with someone new, I felt that I was about to be rejected, that the person would turn away, and that I would be shunned. I felt terrible. As soon as I met someone and started talking, invariably I would have to mention someone's name, which meant that I would have to say the word. Before I said it, I'd hesitate as if I were about to stutter, and I don't even stutter — ever! I am never at a loss for words. But now I couldn't pronounce the word. I'd made a commitment to play the game so I steeled myself and by sheer force of will I said it: *white*. As soon as I said the word, the other person's face would pickle. Right away, very defensively, I'd say, "Oh, I'm playing the Race Game" and try to explain what it was all about. The other person found an excuse to leave as quickly as possible. Each experience was so awful that for two days I forgot that I was supposed to do it. It was a miserable experience.

As Douglas described his experiences, he blushed — frequently. By inviting Douglas to play the Race Game, I had asked him to uncover *his* own feelings about his self-definition as a white. The feeling Douglas uncovered was shame — an acute sense of exposure, loss of trust, abandonment, and humiliation that, as Helen Merrell

Lynd notes in her book *On Shame and the Search for Identity*, are hallmarks of this emotional state.[12]

A point of comparison is in order. Douglas's feelings of being shunned and deserted as a consequence of playing the Race Game are in line with the fears of ostracism described in the personal accounts presented earlier in this chapter. Jackie realized that by inadvertently crossing a color line she had upset her parents. Sally knew better than to rebel when her parents prevented her from dating a black boy. But these earlier stories differ from Douglas's in the crucial sense that the child *did not choose* to call attention to its white racial identity. Nor did it even have one to call attention to.

Dorothy, for example, took on a white racial identity by not playing with the Mexican children, not by choice but out of obedience. As a child, she *had* to obey her parents or face the consequences: the risk of further emotional abandonment and perhaps even physical punishment. Imagine what would have happened to Dorothy if she had repeatedly defied her parents' proscription and played with the Mexican children. (During the entire five-year period of investigation for this book, I met only one Euro-American who, as a child, repeatedly defied her parents' wishes by playing with the "colored" kids on the block. This woman, as it turns out, left home when she was sixteen and is now an expatriate living in Paris.)

Unlike Dorothy and the others, then, Douglas *chose* to step outside the fenced-in area of his community. He *knew* that what he was about to do entailed big risks. He simply steeled himself and by sheer force of will overrode all of his internal warning signals and said the word: *white*. This took courage. We have only to remember the letter from the Euro-American woman explaining why she had been unable to follow through on her own commitment to play the game: she lacked the courage. Douglas was aware of the risks. Nevertheless, shame hit him like a Mack truck. What had happened?

Douglas was hit from two different directions at once: from the outside and the inside. Feelings of both guilt and shame overtook him.

Douglas felt guilt because of what he *did*. He violated an unspoken "gentleman's agreement" between Euro-Americans who are not self-proclaimed white supremacists. To understand this point more precisely, we must become clearer about what the Race Game actually does: it humiliates by publicly exposing feelings associated with becoming white, and it also violates the ground rules for discourse

between Euro-Americans who are not white supremacists. The Race
Game commits this twofold affront in the following way.

To begin, the Race Game describes one Euro-American to another
using the racial ascription *white*. This has a quite different effect
from describing a fellow Euro-American as an ethnic type (e.g., Scot)
or a color type (e.g., blond) or even a bodily type (e.g., short and
squat). The use of the term *white* as a *racial* category in speech by
one Euro-American to another Euro-American presumes that important information about the person being spoken of — and about the
speaker and the listener — is being relayed or at least affirmed by
the ascription.

This presumption, however, countermands a general assumption held by Euro-Americans for whom being white is not a conscious part of their personal identity structure (e.g., Dorothy). Like
Dorothy, most of the Euro-Americans I interviewed did not think
of themselves as white. The category has little *conscious* personal
meaning for them. Rather, like Dorothy, they reserve racial descriptions for persons who are *not* white. Such descriptions say, in effect,
that the person described is not one of us, not part of *our* white
community but, rather, an outsider (e.g., black). But the claim "our
white community" is hidden. It is the "unsaid" in the conversation
as a result of a kind of gentleman's agreement about the limits of
permissible topics for discourse. The Race Game breaks this coded
way of framing reality. It says, in effect, that X is just like us, the
normative community: white. Not only does the speaker turn herself
or himself into an outsider because she or he has broken an unstated
but fully present assumption — racial exclusivity — but, by explic-
itly acting as if her or his listener is also white, the speaker threatens
to expose a hidden truth: neither the speaker nor the listener feels
white enough.

We must remember the actual emotional content of the term
*white* — specifically, the feeling of being at risk within one's own
community because one has committed (or might commit) a com-
munally proscribed act.[13] Such an act threatens emotional perdition:
the loss of the affection of one's caretakers and/or community of
peers. The child and then the adult learn how to suppress such risky
feelings of camaraderie with persons beyond the community's racial
pale in order to decrease the possibility of being exiled from their
own community. And added to the loss of these feelings is the loss of
self-respect resulting from discarding them.

Douglas felt shame because he now faced the feelings he had discarded in order to form his white identity. He thus felt incongruous with his own conscious self-identity. He had discovered feelings that did not cohere with his own sense of himself. This disjunction in self-awareness is the place of a small death, the death of an unadorned feeling. Here we find the relegation of a desire, the disappearance of an embrace, the emotional remains of a rejection as tiny as a "never mind," an unloved part of the self transformed into the feeling of being unlovable. Psychoanalytic theorist Léon Wurmser brings home this point in *The Mask of Shame* when he suggests that "[*b*]*asic shame is the pain of essential unlovability.* It is beyond speech. Ibsen called it the crime of 'soul murder' — this bringing about of unlovability." Shame is the death of an unloved part of the self because it, apparently, is just not good enough to be loved. As Wurmser notes, "The basic flaw for which one is ultimately ashamed is this painful wound: 'I have not been loved because I am at the core unlovable — and I never shall be loved.'"[14]

This denial of one's own feelings in order to be loved is affirmed by one's community and, as something psychologically familiar, tends to *become* a personal value.[15] These personal values are embedded in the child's group values. Collectively, these personal and group values become the basis for developing "a way of living with characteristic codes and beliefs, standards and 'enemies' " to suit the adaptive needs of both the child and its group.[16] When these ways of valuing are overgeneralized, however, they become prejudices against persons and groups who do not fit with this valuational scheme of things.

This definition of prejudice was developed by social psychologist Gordon W. Allport in his classic 1954 work, *The Nature of Prejudice.* My own work affirms Allport's claim that the child cannot help but acquire the suspicions, fears, and hatreds that sooner or later may fix on minority groups because of the ways the child learns these feelings: discipline, love, and threat.[17]

My work, however, is not designed as a study of prejudice or as a discussion about racism or feelings of racial superiority. Rather, I am interested in the way in which the Euro-American child is socialized into a system of values that holds in contempt differences from the white community's ideals. It is this focus on difference that I want to emphasize because when this difference is denied, we find an injury to one's core sense of self that is hidden from view when our attention turns entirely to the way in which *prejudice* is learned and transmitted. The Euro-American child learns to feel ashamed of its own differences from its community's white racial values. By focusing on these feelings of shame, we can find our way back to the site of an injury to the child's sense of self: an attack against the child by members of its own white community because the child is not yet white.

I believe that this racial attack on the Euro-American child must be both acknowledged and addressed if we are to understand the "culture of shame" that pervades Euro-American communities.[18] This shame stems from a fundamental sense of unacceptablity in the eyes of others and an essential sense of separateness and isolation from one's own community of caretakers and peers.[19] These patterns cannot be fully understood until both the source and the nature of the injury to the Euro-American are more adequately understood. The Race Game is one way to get conscious access to this racial injury because it exposes feelings that had to be set aside in order to stop the racial attack against the child by members of its own white community.

Exposing these denied feelings is the second affront brought on by someone who plays the Game. Both parties, initially unaware of the threatening feelings associated with the term *white*, inexplicably feel at risk of being exposed once the Game has begun. They feel, in a word, the onset of shame. Acutely uncomfortable, they scramble for safety. They flee the scene because the information uncovered, the facts threatening to break into (rational) consciousness, is not about their "race." Rather, the exposed feelings pertain to the failures the persons felt in their own formative years within their own caretaking communities — experiences from which they have yet to recover. As these persons become adults, these failures feel like moral failures that threaten self-worth.

The Race Game unearths proscribed feelings and, as such, is a trespass. To play the Game, one has to violate limits and break boundaries. One must step outside the rules for whiteness by disinterring one's own feelings. Such a dig requires a step into the dark. Rather than take this step and "go dark," both Douglas and his conversation partner fled the scene and retreated into the privacy of themselves. They chose to avoid the darkness of this place that lay between them. The Race Game spotlights this dark, foreboding place of cast-off desires. If, in addition to indicting the speaker and listener, the Game succeeds in indicting their families and communities because they were not-quite-good-enough[20] to raise a child as human rather than white, this indictment simply makes the players feel worse. Because it publicly exposes one's experience of becoming white, the Game is intolerable. It is, in a word, shameful because it reveals the differences within the child that it had to deny in order to become congruent with its own caretaking environment. This induction process of the Euro-American child into whiteness is costly.

The child must begin to separate itself from its own feelings. This process of "self-alienation" can leave the child with a sense of "emptiness, futility, or homelessness," which are the hallmarks of psychological child abuse described by psychoanalytic theorist Alice Miller in her book *Prisoners of Childhood: The Drama of the Gifted Child and the Search for the True Self.*[21] It is this sense of being separated from one's own feelings of resonant camaraderie with one's own caretakers and peers, as a white identity is formed, that we must now explore more deeply.

# TWO

# ABUSE

The stories in chapter 1 recount the formation of white racial identities as small but not inconsequential personal defeats. They reveal tiny divestments of personal differences so as to retain the invested interests of one's caretakers or peers. These emotional divestments can be as tiny as a stifled inclination, as measured as a retreat from desire, as constricted as a fenced-in feeling, as minor as a broken date, as earth-shattering as expelling a frat house chum, or as off-putting as an inadvertent stutter. However large or small these divestments feel, no one in these stories drowned; no one was beaten; no one died.

From this subjective perspective, these are not stories about white racism, privilege, or race pride. They are stories about children and adults who learned how to think of themselves as white in order to stay out of trouble with their caretakers and in the good graces of their peers or the enforcers of community racial standards. Their motive was not to attack someone outside their own racial community. They simply wanted to remain within their own community — or at least not to be abandoned by it. They achieved their wish but at a price: the quiet breakup of their core sense of themselves as different from their own community's racial ideals — so quiet that no one noticed that the wholehearted presence of the child or adult was gone.

Again, I shall recount stories of the formation of a white identity, but here I will stress the resulting loss of a sense of difference. My underlying motive remains the same as in chapter 1: to understand the feelings of loss and dismay entailed in becoming white. I don't think the term *white racial abuse* is too strong for what happens in these stories.

## White America's First Racial Victim: Its Own Child

My first story comes from an op-ed essay by the Los Angeles–based writer Don Wallace published in the October 11, 1995, *New York Times*. In the essay, titled "How I Learned to Fear the Cops," Wallace describes several incidents in which he was accosted by the police.[1] Wallace uses the term *the nonwhite zone* to identify the geographic locale of these altercations, but the term could also include the subjective location within himself where the resulting fear and submissive adjustments to brute police authority took up residence.

The first altercation occurred when Wallace was ten. A police officer drew his gun on the boy because he was a white kid playing in a brown part of Los Angeles. Wallace uses the third-person singular to tell this tale in the opening paragraphs of his essay:

> The 10-year-old boy skipped down the sidewalk a few steps ahead of his parents in the warmth of a Los Angeles night in 1962. Behind him glowed Olvera Street, a slice of the old California's Mexican heritage.... He heard the screech of brakes but paid no mind until a police officer seized him by the shoulder and pushed him against a wall. Another officer shoved his 12-year-old brother. Then the boy saw something even more terrifying: the gun in the cop's hand.

Wallace's father spoke up, berating the policeman for daring to take out his gun in the presence of his sons and demanding an apology for pointing a gun at his sons, who were churchgoers, Boy and Cub Scout members, and good students. The cops stood their ground, demanding that the father get out of the way or face arrest. Wallace, who until this point has not told the reader the race of the family, now teases his reader, asking: "What do you think happened next? You've read the papers. You followed the Rodney King case. If the family in this true story were black, what odds would you give on the father staying out of jail? Or staying alive." But he and his family are white, Wallace tells us, and they "got to go home to [their] all-white suburb."[2]

Wallace tells this story in a tone at once bemused and cocky.

As a teenager, Wallace continued to play on the wrong side of town. He attended a large, inner-city high school in Long Beach and would often visit his first girlfriend, "a biology whiz" who had a Spanish surname and lived on the West Side. To visit her,

Wallace had to go through a Checkpoint Charlie consisting of a concrete levee, oil fields, and two eight-lane boulevards marking a racial
change from all-white to brown, black, and yellow. The few streets
that led in or out of the area created choke points and were usually
"guarded by a squad car at each [point], day and night."

In his sophomore year, almost every night as he drove from his
girlfriend's house, a squad car would swing behind him and tail him.
"I got used to it," Wallace says with the determination of a teenage
Rambo. He treated "each drive home as if it were a mission through
hostile territory: my signals perfect, my turns crisp, my speed steady
and always five miles per hour below the limit." Nevertheless, in
spite of his white, "preppie look," he was stopped eleven times "with
nary a ticket to show for it." The policemen's message was clear:
whites were not allowed to socialize in a nonwhite zone. Recounting
an incident in which he and two friends were caught in the wrong
zone, Wallace writes:

> [T]he police marched three of us into a field behind a screen of
> oil wells and then separated and handcuffed us. For an hour we
> were threatened with a beating and arrest, yet no infraction was
> mentioned. The police were delivering their message of intim-
> idation, insuring the crackle of fear, the walking-on-eggshells
> feeling, every time we entered the nonwhite zone.

Similarly, when Wallace, who was president of the student body and
a football letterman, chose to sit with black friends during a school
basketball game, two police officers "waded into the bleachers and
hauled me out to the floor to be searched, in full view of my teachers
and friends." Such incidents made it clear not only that race-mixing
was prohibited by these cops but that neither whites nor nonwhites
were safe from police brutality when they entered a racial zone off-
limits to their kind. There is, however, another story being told.
Wallace, in the process of recounting his youthful escapades with the
police, also sings a different tune. He tells us how "this white boy
[who] got the message long ago" grew up to "fear the cops." Wallace
recounts this adult tale of submission to authority in another key.

Wallace's journalistic eye focuses our attention on the reality that
as a youth, in spite of his ostensible rebellious nature, he did not
rebel. The boy did not protest his harassment but adjusted. Writes
Wallace: "I am astonished how we adjusted to this state of constant
siege." This adult astonishment forces us to set aside his teenage

bravado and focus on a fact that neither the teenager nor the adult could state directly: both the white youth *and* white adult civilians in Wallace's recollections submitted to the policemen's harassment.

That he submitted to authority is clear. We simply must pay attention to the unsaid. Absent from Wallace's account is a description of complaints to his parents or schoolteachers. Nor does he report having gone either to the local police station or to the district attorney's office to file a complaint. Such acts would have been made less likely by the fact that both his parents and the adults at his school were models of submission to police abuse rather than rebellion. Even Wallace's father, after an initial dismayed protest against the officer who had pulled a gun on white boys who were good (Scouts, Christian, and smart), relented and took his family home to their "all-white suburb." This, of course, was what the cops had in the first place desired. Wallace thus describes the antics of a teenager who grandstanded rather than rebelled.

Wallace is thus not simply telling us about members of a police force out of control. He is also exposing the pervasive white adult submission to the threatening presence of its own police force, which is dead set on preventing race-mixing. The adult submission to this threat, in the boy's eyes, was the same as consent. The police harassment *plus* the massive submission of the adults to this brute force *together* taught the boy, and the adult he grew into, what he must do to act like a white person: submit to the unwritten race laws of his policed state. This demand for submission to white race laws created a zone of fear and timidity within Wallace, the adult. As he writes: "Layer upon layer of incidents like these build a foundation of mistrust. It's why I'm a very cautious driver today." Wallace, in effect, has described the origins of his present siege mentality.

As Wallace learned through experience, *in a de jure and/or de facto system of racial apartheid, every member of the Euro-American community is under siege.* Not even children are protected from the long arm of the law if they violate America's race laws. As a result of the layering process described by Wallace, he developed an adult "walking-on-eggshells feeling" that I call his *internal nonwhite zone.* In this zone, his fear of the police was hardened into an attitude that turned him into an overly cautious driver who has adjusted his actions to accommodate himself to life in a racial police state.

This siege mentality prevents Wallace from expressing rage toward the police force even in his essay. Instead of calling for more civilian oversight of an out-of-control police force, Wallace muffles his impulse to protest by cloaking it in blackness and concludes his essay with the moral tepidity of an interracial truism: "I firmly believe there will be no peace until black people can walk the same streets as white people without fearing the sound of the squad car's brakes, as I learned to do that night on Olvera Street." By referring to the risk African Americans run when they enter white zones, Wallace expresses in blackface his own fears of being caught in the wrong racial zone.

Wallace's essay is thus a description of one way in which a social system of racial apartheid is maintained by members of a city's police force: the intimidation of a Euro-American child who learns firsthand that no white adult will protect him from this brute force. This kind of racially induced fear, as we saw in chapter 1, does not usually originate with the threat of violence, as represented for Wallace by a policeman's gun. Such a graphic display is not usually necessary because the community's racial induction strategies and socialization processes have already succeeded in deadening the child's desire to venture into the nonwhite zones of Euro-American life. To find evidence of the pervasive nature of this deadening process, we have only to recall Dan's eighth-grade graduation trip through the South, when he learned not to voice questions about the "colored" and "white" signs because not even the teachers murmured a word of protest or explanation.

In the face of adult silence to racial abuse, the child learns to silence and then deny its own resonant feelings toward racially proscribed others, not because it chooses to become white, but because it wishes to remain within the community that is quite literally its life. The child thus learns, "layer by layer," to stay away from the nonwhite zones of its own desires.

The internal nonwhite zone is the killing fields of desire, the place where impulses to community with persons beyond the pale are slaughtered. The child develops an antipathy toward its own forbidden feelings *and* to the persons who are the objects of these forbidden desires: the racial other. This developing white attitude in the child is a "means of being 'ready' and 'set' to act in a certain way."[3]

Most very young Euro-American children, for example, have not yet learned to avoid making African American friends or to think of such persons as inferior.[4] Such community values are not yet in place.

The child has not yet learned the words and values that its community links to the sentient set-asides of personal feeling the child has already commenced to practice. Rather, the child simply has an emotional predisposition to develop such a racial lexicon of values — later. This predisposition is present because it is the abstracted patterning principles that express the child's pattern of setting aside its own resonant feelings toward persons racially despised by the child's own community. The resulting patterning principles of these set-asides are the ground for later symbolic formation of a value-laden racial lexicon.[5] Each of these affective set-asides accomplished by the child can contribute to the development of an attitude that will function for the child like a cocked gun — "the person and the gun are thereafter poised for action." Soon the child will learn to fire the racial salvo that reduces a human being to a despised racial object.[6] In a word, the child who first learned to say, "Mama, see the Negro! I'm frightened!"[7] will soon be able to say, "Look at the nigger!...Mama, a Negro!"[8]

Only from this vantage point of the incremental loss of feeling can we begin to both discern and explain why *all* of the adults in Wallace's high school gym sat passively as they watched a white teenager be harassed by white policemen for race-mixing. The first level of their restraint from moral action, I would argue, came not from racial hatred but from fear. The next level came from their own racial antipathy toward race-mixing learned as the articulated, value-laden fallout from this fear.

Wallace's use of the term *nonwhite zone* is particularly potent because it actually refers to three overlapping areas of white self-definition: (1) the psychic region that separates the self from its own feelings of positive resonance toward racially proscribed others and its negative sentiment toward its own white community for preventing the positive feelings toward the forbidden "other" from being expressed; (2) the residential ghettos to which the vast majority of the colored residents are invariably consigned in an American city or town;[9] and (3) the field of interplay between the child's subjective, inner world and the surrounding objective, outer world beyond it. In this interpersonal field of interplay, the child learns through interaction with its caretakers what feelings to embrace and what feelings to reject in order to retain the affection of its caretakers.

The nonwhite zone thus refers to three regions: inner, outer, and between. Objectively, it is the place where one goes for actual con-

tact with racially proscribed persons. Subjectively, it is the point
of contact within the self where forbidden desires are felt and denied.[10] Interpersonally, it is the place where "layer upon layer," one's
environment teaches one to suppress forbidden feelings and desires.

In sum, the first internal referent for the nonwhite zone in Euro-
American life is the self's own proscribed feelings. The third referent
has a source that is both external and internal, or between the self
and its world: its interactions with its own white community of caretakers. The second referent for the nonwhite zone pertains to the
nonwhite ghetto in an American city, town, or suburb. Not surprisingly, this distinct residential zone in an area becomes associated
with the fear, sense of loss and dismay, and rage lodged in the
Euro-American's internal nonwhite zone. The concrete ghetto thus
becomes an objective symbol for both the Euro-American's racial
fears and her or his lost desires for a community that does not judge
but embraces difference as good. The lure of the nonwhite zones
of American cities thus gains its power of attraction from repressed
desires looking for a way to escape their white confines.

The nonwhite zone must be vigilantly patrolled, then, for along its
border lies the terrain of race-mixing. Like any line that seems to distinguish one thing from another, upon careful scrutiny, one discovers
the line is porous; it is perforated. That which is ostensibly excluded
by the line is in fact included. The line thus marks the place where
ostensibly distinct, discrete phenomena meet. It is where the "interplay of differences" occurs.[11] Here, race-mixing takes place in the
fantasies of real life. Forbidden desire merges with fear and trans-
forms the nonwhite zone into a red light district that both attracts
and barricades the white passerby to her or his own desires.

Flannery O'Connor captures this feeling of frightening fascination
and repulsed desire in Euro-American life toward racial others as
she describes the attraction of a young southern white boy named
Nelson to a large colored woman leaning in a doorway:

> He stood drinking in every detail of her. His eyes traveled up
> from her great knees to her forehead and then made a triangu-
> lar path from the glistening sweat on her neck down and across
> her tremendous bosom and over her bare arm back to where
> her fingers lay hidden in her hair. He suddenly wanted her to
> reach down and pick him up and draw him against her and
> then he wanted to feel her breath on his face. He wanted to

look down and down into her eyes while she held him tighter and tighter. He had never had such a feeling before. He felt as if he were reeling down through a pitchblack tunnel....

Nelson would have collapsed at her feet if Mr. Head [his white guardian for the day] had not pulled him roughly away. ...They hurried down the street and Nelson did not look back at the woman. He pushed his hat sharply forward over his face which was already burning with shame.[12]

Such feelings of shame are a kind of final defense mechanism used to hide proscribed impulses from the threats of one's caretakers.[13] Shame acts as a kind of Checkpoint Charlie for the elements in Euro-American life that induce white racial fear and loathing when they appear. White shame functions as a psychological guard, as an L.A. cop whose sole duty is to keep the emotions of the residents of this realm in check. This effort entails a protracted battle. When a forbidden feeling manages a furtive escape and comes to the fore as race-mixing or rage toward one's own white community, white shame and fear strong-arm it back into place by deadening feeling and extinguishing desire anew. The success of the strategy renders the original injury invisible. No gun is needed; no veiled threat of the withdrawal of love is required. The child has learned to police its own forbidden impulses to community. The child submits; the teenager postures rebellion; the adult, when it glimpses its true state, expresses astonishment that it has adjusted so fittingly to a constant state of siege.

•

In addition to the policing of racial borders, white racial abuse against Euro-Americans also takes the form of a Euro-American pecking order among ethnic groups. As Gordon Allport writes, this scheme is widespread and remarkably uniform in judgments "concerning the relative acceptability [i.e., whiteness] of various ethnic stocks: Germans, Italians, Armenians, and the like. Each of these can in sequence look down upon all groups lower in the series."[14] Racial abuse meted out to Euro-Americans who are too far from the Anglo-Saxon Protestant can have devastating effects on personality.

Psychoanalytic theorist Andrew P. Morrison presents a classic description of these effects in his case study of a "Mr. Relling,"[15] who "felt great shame and humiliation over his ethnic background, and expended much effort trying to present himself as a WASP from a prominent lineage." Writes Morrison:

> Mr. Relling gradually described how ashamed both of his parents had been about their ethnic origins, how both had changed their names — including his mother's middle name, which she altered to suggest a shared lineage with a prominent Yankee politician. "How could I do otherwise?" he lamented. At this question I raised my eyebrows, and wondered aloud whether he felt inevitably destined to repeat his parent's self-disdain.[16]

Morrison's analysis, however, overlooks the racial component in Mr. Relling's shame: the fact that he is not white enough. When Morrison discusses race he restricts himself to interracial conflicts and intraracial issues within oppressed, racial minority communities. For him, race pertains to "racism" and the "racism-poverty-shame shackle" found in black America's urban ghettos. When he links race and shame, he is referring to "black" shame and "institutional oppression." Accordingly, Morrison's analysis of Mr. Relling's condition cannot take into account the racial component of his own client's oppression; the one concept that could identify such racial abuse is missing: white shame. Thus, when Morrison lists the "various guises" that can conceal shame, including rage, contempt, envy, and depression, he overlooks the guise of whiteness as a self-degrading system of identity formation.[17]

Morrison rightly suggests that America's pervasive violence results from American society's failure to redress widespread inequities and humiliations. But by overlooking the shame entailed in becoming white in America, he ignores white violence against Euro-Americans and cannot suggest ways to end it. Before this racial abuse within white communities can be addressed, it must first be seen. For this purpose, I turn to the Jewish American writer Norman Podhoretz's recollections of becoming white in America.

## Norman Podhoretz's White Problem

The autobiographical reflections of Norman Podhoretz, the neoconservative pundit and editor at large of *Commentary* magazine, provide a vivid account of the abuse suffered within white America by Euro-Americans who are not Anglo-Saxon Protestants but nevertheless want to "make it" in WASP culture and society.

In his book *Making It*, Podhoretz acknowledges that the American social contract he repeatedly faced as a lower-class Jewish student from Brooklyn who wanted the class privileges and securities of *goyish* American high culture and society demanded that he become a "facsimile WASP." In the process, he learned to feel ashamed of his own parents' immigrant, eastern European, Orthodox Jewish manners, mannerisms, speech patterns, and lifestyle. But he did not break ranks with "the family," the New York Jewish intelligentsia, for he ultimately "made it" into the "American" realm of power, privilege, and prestige as a *Jew*, not as a facsimile WASP. Podhoretz's own overview of the white racial induction process he had to endure is worth quoting at length. As Podhoretz notes:

> [W]hile class in America certainly had as much to do with money as in England, it also had to do — in a way for which England offered no parallel — with the question of whether or not one had been born white, Protestant, and of Anglo-Saxon ancestry, and had been raised, of course, accordingly.
>
> One could, as I had already learned, become a facsimile WASP: that much open to talent the American upper class actually was and that far its egalitarianism clearly did extend. But unless one succeeded in turning oneself into such a person, one was unlikely to become eligible for a whole range of the powers and privileges America had to offer. For the American social contract — on which, as with the primordial social contract itself, the peace of so divided and fragmented a society rested — had been implicitly extended in the post–Civil War period to cover the problems presented by the influx of millions of immigrants with their strange tongues, their peasant customs, their "barbaric" and "uncivilized" ways. And the contract was this: to the degree that these people would submit to "Americanization" — which is to say, to the degree that they would learn and adopt the language, traditions, and customs of the oldest American group — to that degree would they be "accepted" — which is to say, freed from *some* of the many kinds of discrimination, gross and subtle, open and concealed, to which, in defiance of the strictly legal social contract called

the Constitution, that presumably governed the country, they were invariably and cruelly subjected.[18]

Podhoretz did not want to submit to this Americanization process and become a facsimile WASP, but he did. A case in point is his story of the way in which his WASP high school teacher "Mrs. K." tried to break his ethnic Jewish, eastern European ways so that he could gain entrée to an Ivy League school. Through this careful tutelage and his own self-described drive for self-esteem, he did gain entrée to Columbia College in the 1940s, when its Jewish quota system was still firmly in place. Podhoretz's "confession stories" are thus, in effect, tales of his battle with himself over whether to be or not to be a facsimile WASP.

He refers to this internal battle in his 1979 book, *Breaking Ranks: A Political Memoir,* in which he also admits that when the radical white student and women's movements of the 1960s threatened his hard-earned place in "the establishment," he broke ranks with the left and turned right.[19] This break, however, was foreshadowed sixteen years earlier in his February 1963 essay "My Negro Problem — and Ours," published in *Commentary.* In it, Podhoretz describes how Jewish and Italian children in his lower-class Brooklyn neighborhood were united as "whites" by their shared experience of persecution by local "Negro boys." He is thus appalled by the current belief among his liberal white friends and colleagues that all Negroes should evoke sympathy because *they* are persecuted. To counter this racial myth of universal black suffering, Podhoretz presents a barrage of personal accounts of the ways in which *he,* as a child in the 1930s, was repeatedly "beaten up, robbed, and in general hated, terrorized, and humiliated" by the Negroes in his Brooklyn neighborhood.[20] Thirty years after these incidents, Podhoretz, the self-identified "liberal," confesses that in spite of his present enlightened views about race, he still hates and envies Negroes. These feelings, he acknowledges, are now mixed with "twinges of fear and the resentment they bring and the self-contempt they arouse," but he concludes that all "American whites," whether they have had personally harrowing experiences with black Americans or not, nevertheless, like him, "are sick in their feelings about Negroes."

By acknowledging that his own feelings of white ethnic shame are mixed in with his resentment toward Negroes, Podhoretz begins to mask his own white ethnic shame issues as an interracial "Negro problem." He admits, for example, that he resented the Negro boys' refusal to submit to the rules of the white world to which he had already begun to acquiesce. This confession is made all the more complex by Podhoretz's awareness that even if the Negro boys who harassed him in his childhood Brooklyn neighborhood had submitted to the WASP rules for success, they would have had slim chance of "making it" in the same way that was open to him because he, when contrasted with them, was white. Negro submission en masse was thus virtually pointless.

The Negro, Podhoretz observes, thus

> feared the impulses within himself toward submission to authority no less powerfully than I feared the impulses in myself toward defiance. If I represented the jailer to him, it was not because I was oppressing him or keeping him down: it was because I symbolized for him the dangerous and probably pointless temptation toward greater repression, just as he symbolized for me the equally perilous tug toward greater freedom. I personally was to be rewarded for this repression with a new and better life in the future, but how many of my friends paid an even higher price and were given only gall in return.

What did Podhoretz "repress" about himself in order to achieve his "new and better life"? Parts of his own ethnic social history and genealogy. Podhoretz admits that

- the very idea of his high school teacher Mrs. K. meeting his mother filled him with shame because his mother had a Yiddish accent.[21]

- he did not rail against Mrs. K., who despised her middle-class Jewish students even more than she despised her "slum children," nor would he protest her "bantering gibes at [his] parents," even when her words made him blush.

- in retrospect, he realizes that he was learning that "there was no socially neutral ground to be found in the United States of America, and that a distaste for the surroundings in which I was bred, and ultimately (God forgive me) even for many of the people I loved, and so a new taste for other kinds of people" was required if he were going to "make it."[22]

Podhoretz, in effect, acknowledges that he had indeed begun to perceive himself as a "Jew" from the standpoint of the gentile, upper-class world. From this vantage point, Podhoretz became "different" and "other" to the *white* world. This is the stuff of Jewish self-hatred. As Sander L. Gilman painstakingly demonstrates in his book *Jewish Self-Hatred,* this self-contempt is achieved through the use of personal self-identity definitions provided by a world that despises Jews. In Europe, such definition meant that the Jew could be thought of as black. As Gilman notes, "In the eyes of the non-Jew who defined them in Western [European] society the Jews became the blacks."[23] The male Jew and the male African were conceived of as equivalent threats to the white race.[24] Did Podhoretz's own Jewish self-hatred suggest this European paradigm? Did he become a Negro Jew to himself?

Evidence for this conflation is found in Podhoretz's own description of the "tears of rage" he felt toward the Negro boys who humiliated him as a child in his Brooklyn neighborhood and the "self-contempt" he felt as a result of this humiliation. He freely admits that these boys represented for him "the very embodiment of the values of the street" that he had abandoned: the boys were "free, independent, reckless, brave, masculine, erotic." They were "beautifully, enviably tough, not giving a damn for anyone or anything" — all the things that Podhoretz, in his own eyes, was not and dared not give into: the perilous tug toward greater freedom from the WASP rule.[25]

The impulse toward rebellion and freedom from this white rule, however, clearly threatened Podhoretz's stronger desire to make it in a world that despised his ethnic differences from the WASP ideal. He thus "feared this impulse in [himself] toward defiance" and suppressed it, thereby thwarting his own efforts at a cohesive, personal integration and self-definition. The resulting challenge to his own internal self-integrity represented by his thwarted desires to greater freedom felt like an inner death threat and produced rage, which is a violent impulse to stave off the feeling of jeopardy brought on by the collapse of self-coherence.[26] If we consider that "Negroes" represent a threat to Podhoretz's own sense of self-coherence, we can understand his characterization of his own "rage" against Negro anti-Semites as "insane." When he simply *thinks* about this problem, he goes into an "insane rage."[27] His hysterics pertain to his anti-Semitic feelings against himself, which signal his own inner death as a coherent self. In short, he hates himself for hating himself.

In this skewed scenario, the Negro anti-Semite becomes a mask: the blackface of Podhoretz's own white shame. His rage against the Negro masks his own white shame (or his own Jewish anti-Semitism) by making it unrecognizable. Such a strategy is in keeping with shame, which "forces one to hide, to seek cover and to veil or mask oneself." Shame conceals the threat of external punishment to the self (e.g., from Mrs. K. and the WASP world) by replacing this external threat with the self's own internal feelings of humiliation, scorn, and contempt.[28] Podhoretz thus displayed his own inner death brought on by his suppressed impulses toward freedom (shame) to prevent an attack from the WASP world (white racial abuse) by expressing an "insane rage" against Negroes (white racism) who represented the freedom he had lost. Their freedom became the target of his rage and thus a mask for his shame.[29]

Or perhaps Negro anti-Semitism simply exposed Podhoretz's vulnerability as a white with a low ethnic status in the Euro-American pecking order. Even if this is so, however, Podhoretz's "insane rage" against Negro anti-Semites still is a mask of shame:[30] more precisely, white shame expressed as the feeling of not being white enough.

The intensity of his rage and his other so-called sick feelings toward Negroes suggests that Podhoretz had entered the nonwhite zone of his own white identity. As with Don Wallace, this place was built up in Podhoretz layer upon layer as assaults on his behavior continued because of his difference from the values of a white ideal.

What is of particular interest to us in this discussion is not what other whites did to Podhoretz but the way in which he internalized the assaults and affirmed the rectitude of their degrading treatment of him. This transformation of others' contempt into self-contempt is the signature of shame. When the original contempt has its origins in white racial antipathy toward whites who are ethnically not quite white enough, the turn of this contempt inward is white ethnic shame.

When we remove the black mask behind which Podhoretz conceals his white ethnic shame, we do not find an interracial issue between blacks and whites but an intraracial issue between Euro-Americans deemed not to be white enough and their white racial assailants. Podhoretz gives us a particularly raw image of the white abuse entailed in his induction into the ranks of whiteness as a facsimile WASP — the "dirty little secret" of his white world — when recounting his own self-deprecating reaction to his friends' envious taunts after he won a Fulbright fellowship to study in England:

> It was the first time I had ever experienced the poisoning of success by envy. Because it was the envy not of enemies but of friends, and because it came to me not naked and undisguised but posing as love and masked in ideologically plausible rationalizations, it was hard to identify as envy — and harder still because in my instinctive terror of becoming the object of this expropriating and cannibalistic passion, I was unwilling to admit to myself that it was in fact being directed against me. And no doubt in my terror of it, I was also trying to ward the envy off by allowing my friends to make me so miserable that they would finally have nothing to envy me for. Theirs the virtue of failure, mine the corruption of success: who then was the enviable one?
>
> With all this, my introduction to the dirty little secret of our age was more or less complete.[31]

In this passage, Podhoretz's use of the word *terror* to describe his feelings of having his ethnic identity expropriated and consumed is appropriate. The "little secret" of having to become a facsimile WASP in order to make it, as Podhoretz discovered, is "dirty" because a facsimile is a lie. He was indeed experiencing the death of himself as someone with a coherent, cohesive personal history and identity as both white and ethnic. Manners, education, and erudition, he discovered, are not enough to make one a true WASP. Pedigree also pertains to ethnicity and is bred into the child as part of its cultural heritage. To acquire the pedigree in any other way turns one into a posturing pretense, a WASP manqué, a facsimile WASP: someone who is living a lie. Psychoanalysis can identify this shame problem but as of yet lacks an adequate concept to discuss the racial component entailed in the breakup of the self's own integrity: *white* abuse against the non-WASP aspects of a Euro-American's racial identity. Yet one thing is certain: such abuse is racist.

•

As we saw in chapter 1, an early stage entailed in becoming white for many Euro-American children is the experience of setting aside feelings that are not empathically affirmed by the racial interests of their own caretaking community. From this perspective, white ethnic shame pertains to the unmirrored, split-off parts of the white self-identity. These aspects of the self are the cultural patterns of engagement and display of mannerisms and style that do not fit the "high-culture" WASP ideal that Podhoretz and "Mr. Relling" aspired to emulate. Psychoanalytic shame theorist Donald L. Nathanson graphically describes this high-culture ideal in contrast to his own self-caricatured ethnic ways:

> Look what happens if I take on the role of a sophisticated, urbane, upperclass WASP gentleman. Shelved, for the moment, will be my own more characteristic ebullience and the tendency to wave my arms as...I warm to my subject. My body will be held in a relaxed and easy-going posture; everything about me will suggest that I am in command. My facial set will be one you might describe as "sensitive"; when upset I will tend to turn away in a mild demonstration of reticence.... Brought to the fore will be such mannerisms as an air of utter restraint, a debonair and condescending attitude of uninvolvement... in the antics of what are now defined as "lesser folk," and a certain highly stylized set of attitudes toward nearly everything, all expressed with considerable economy of gesture. Maturity, for me, will be displayed in terms of relaxed self-confidence.... The overwhelming weight of evidence suggests that such behavior is trained into us during childhood by a culture or subculture with highly specific rules for the display and control of innate affect.[32]

It is well worth noting here that Nathanson acknowledges that his own personal experience leads him to believe that "most people who seem to 'have it all together' are pretty much fake — enlightenment is for them merely a role to be assumed rather than a state of being."[33] Nevertheless, Nathanson's portrait of the WASP in contradistinction to his own style illustrates my point: if the difference between the white self-image as WASP and as ethnic is too extreme, the ethnic self-image, when exposed, brings on feelings of white shame because the flawed (=ethnic) part of one's own white identity has been revealed. White ethnic shame is the self's *disparagement of its own nonwhite ethnic zone of experience as distinct from the WASP ideal.*

Unless we take Podhoretz's white ethnic shame into account, we cannot possibly understand the complex nature of his antipathy and "sickness" toward "Negroes" because a central element required in this analysis will be missing: the abuse he suffered at the hands of whites that shattered his coherence as an ethnic white and made him rage against Negroes to mask his own white ethnic shame.

The most graphic demonstration of the extent of Podhoretz's terror of his own Jewish identity being "cannibalized" as he is ingested by the WASP world is his proposed solution to the "Negro problem": miscegenation. The Negro must disappear through intermarriage. Writes Podhoretz: "[T]he Negro problem can be solved in this country in no other way."[34] The absurdity of his "final solution" for the Negro was brought home to him by novelist Ralph Ellison, who suggested that such a strategy would simply "increase the number of 'colored' children." Said Podhoretz: this was "a point, I had to admit, which had never occurred to me before."[35] But this point is so obvious that we have to ask ourselves what blinded him to it. My answer is white ethnic shame. The gap in Podhoretz's reasoning indicates the presence of his own terror of death brought on by the collapse of his internal integrity as both white and nonwhite. His solution to the "Negro problem" would get rid of his "white problem" by bringing about the disappearance of the WASP. His resentment at having to submit to the white world's rules also hardens in his mind and heart into the symbol of the Negro boys who terrorized his youth. The original object of this resentment in the white world is "Mrs. K.," who forced him to conform, as best he could, to a WASP social contract. The shame induced by a strategy of self-contempt created a blinding racial resentment against both whites and blacks. Podhoretz concludes his essay with the frank admission that if his daughter wanted "to marry one," he would rail, rave, rant, and then "give her my blessing." Here we find Podhoretz with both his best and his worst foot forward at the same time. He steps forward, simultaneously, as both the racial bigot and the race reformer.[36]

In sum, Podhoretz's Negro problem results from his own self-contempt as a facsimile WASP. This story is told in blackface as his Negro problem, but it is actually the story of his "white problem — and ours." It is the story of the racialization process for Euro-Americans within their own white world of experience that they must undergo in order to attain and sustain class privilege as a right of race. This process entails a white displacement of rage against its WASP world onto African Americans.

Granted, a pervasive and abiding sense of humiliation by African Americans did indeed create a "white" community of Italian and Jewish boys in Podhoretz's youth hostile toward their black assailants. But this community was externally defined by the menacing activity of others instead of internally defined by common customs, traditions, rituals, and shared beliefs by the Jewish and Italian American boys. The actual content of this "white" group was thus their individual private feelings of shame and rage.

As mentioned above, Podhoretz believes that even whites who have not gone through his wrenching boyhood experience of racial attacks by Negroes harbor knotted feelings of rage against blacks and self-contempt. But although such feelings can create a mob, they cannot forge a community. The actual content of such a white group, being purely negative, enjoins the members of the group to act negatively by doing such things as burning bodies, books, and crosses or, at least, blacking up their rage enough to mug an innocent African American passerby.

A third example of white abuse within white communities demonstrates how Euro-American social scientists who analyze ethnic conflicts within white communities overlook this problem of white racial abuse against Euro-Americans. The field work and case studies of working-class Euro-Americans who are not Anglo-Saxon Protestants conducted by social scientists Richard Sennett and Jonathan Cobb and published in their 1972 book, *The Hidden Injuries of Class,* are a case in point. As they attempted to understand the inner turmoil of ethnic workers like Frank Rissaro, who is discussed below, they did not think about Euro-American ethnic conflicts as a white intraracial problem, although that is exactly what they are.

## Frank Rissaro's Invisible Race Problem

Frank Rissaro [a pseudonym], a third-generation Italian-American, forty-four years old when we talked with him, had worked his way up from being a shoeshine boy at the age of nine to classifying loan applications in a bank. He makes $10,000 a year, owns a suburban home, and every August rents a small cottage in the country. He is a man who at first glance

appears satisfied—"I know I did a good job in my life"—and
yet he is also a man who feels defensive about his honor, fearing that people secretly do not respect him; he feels threatened
by his children, who are "turning out just the way I want them
to be," and he runs his home in a dictatorial manner....

[Frank also] feels passive in the midst of his success because
he feels illegitimate, a pushy intruder, in his entrance to the
middle-class world of neat suburban lawns, peaceable families,
happy friendships. Despite the fact that he has gained entrée, he
doesn't believe he deserves to be respected.[37]

When Sennett and Cobb interviewed Frank Rissaro and other
white "ethnic" workers, they discovered a "hidden anxiety" in them:
the belief that they are not fit for a higher rung on the American ladder of success than what they have achieved. The two social scientists
call the social environment that produces this anxiety "a morality
of shaming and self-doubt" and argue that such a morality makes
workers feel that they have no one to blame for their failures except
themselves.[38] Much to the chagrin of the two scholars, the workers
accept their status, that is, arbitrary limits on how high a social rank
they can attain, as legitimate even though they also disapprove of the
division of America into haves and have-nots.

The two scholars discovered that core to the worker's low self-
esteem is a strategy of "self-accusation," which leads the worker
to reason: "If only I had been a better person, I could have made
it." The conundrum, of course, is that this worker knows at the
same time that he never had a chance. Nevertheless, he makes his
class position *his* personal responsibility, even though he also knows
that it is not.[39] This is a shame strategy: the workers blame their
modest attainments on their own unworthiness. Sennett and Cobb
conclude that these workers have internalized their class and mirror
internally the class structure in which they live: a structure that provides no respect for those at the bottom. As a result, an internal class
war is being waged within workers who damn themselves for being
who they are: workers. This pitched inner battle is a hidden injury
of class.[40]

Sennett and Cobb, however, are not as astute about race as they
are about class. First, they fail to notice the white racial identities
of these workers. The social scientists, for instance, note that urban
renewal projects have intruded into these workers' "ethnic" enclaves

and stripped them of their local church, ethnic political machine, and other traditional institutions that gave each neighborhood its own particular cultural and ethnic signature as well as its political clout in the larger white world. Their ethnic communities crumbling, these workers were "forced" to become white. Sennett and Cobb, however, conclude otherwise. They suggest that this "forced integration" in which the Irish or Poles or other "ethnic" groups were melded into one group resulted in their becoming "laborers" or "workers," a new identity that is shameful and humiliating for these men because they lost their "specialness" as ethnics with their own cultures. The final result of this homogenization process, Sennett and Cobb argue, is thus an "average," unexceptional American. Not quite.

For if these workers were not "white," they would not have been able to get housing in the area in which they now live as "Americans."[41] Their ethnicity plays no role in their ability to quite literally "fit" into their white residential environment. They are newly "whited" workers — or at least a part of them. And this is, of course, the problem. Part of them is white, and part of them is "ethnic" (hence Frank Rissaro's description of himself as an intruder in his own suburban neighborhood). Sennett and Cobb also note that the bosses of these workers and the school teachers of the workers' children humiliate them because they lack the "privileges high culture bestows." They have made material gains that are supposed to "melt" them into the American middle class, but they are continually barraged with "impudent snobbery," "shaming," and "putdown." But in reality, this abuse is meted out because these workers are not quite white enough.

This is Sennett and Cobb's second oversight: they ignore the ethnic rating system that determines racial standing within white America. In fact, the social scientists provide a vivid example of this racial issue within Euro-American society without mentioning the role of race:

[At the school attended by the workers' children,] the teachers act on their expectations of the children in such a way as to *make* the expectations [of the teachers] become reality. Here is how the process worked in one second-grade class at Watson School — unusual in that it was taught by a young man. In this class there were two children, Frank and Vincent, whose appearance was somewhat different from that of the others: their

clothes were no fancier than the other children's, but they were
pressed and seemed better kept; in a class of mostly dark Italian children, these were the fairest-skinned. From the outset the
teacher singled out these two children, implying that they most
closely approached his own standards for classroom performance. To them he spoke with a special warmth in his voice. He
never praised them openly by comparison to the other children,
but a message that they were different, were better, was spon-
taneously conveyed. As the observer watched the children play
and work over the course of the school year, he noticed these
two boys becoming more serious, more solemn, as the months
passed. Obedient and never unruly from the first, by the end of
the year they were left alone by the other children.[42]

Sennett and Cobb have described the racial child abuse by the
teacher of his darker students, whose appearance did not fit into
color and neatness categories that mark off a pecking order of gentil-
ity as race status. In the previous discussion of Mrs. K., we saw that
Podhoretz knew what was going on. And he knew that the darker
boys in his neighborhood could not "make it" even if their clothes
were better pressed and their manners were more polite than those
of the white boys on the block. Sennett and Cobb describe the same
kind of racial discrimination in their account of this grade-school
class but without using the category of race, although they describe
the different pigmentations.

This absence of racial analysis from their work prevents them
from adequately understanding the structure and nature of the
"identity crisis" they observed in the workers, who are now

> trying to find out what position they occupy in America as a
> whole.... For the people interviewed, integration into Ameri-
> can life meant integration into a world with different symbols
> of human respect and courtesy, a world in which human ca-
> pabilities are measured in terms profoundly alien to those that
> prevailed in their childhood. The changes in their lives mean
> more to them than a chance, or a failure, to acquire middle-
> class *things*. For them, history is challenging them and their
> children to become "cultured," in the intellectual's sense of that
> word, if they want to achieve respect in the new American
> terms; and toward that challenge they feel deeply ambivalent.[43]

Part of this crisis has to do with being white but not WASP, with the middle-class manners and sensibilities of this ethnic group. Simply stated, Sennett and Cobb have uncovered a *white ethnic identity crisis* as well as a class crisis in the lives of these workers. But the theorists only saw the class issue, never imagining the possibilities that these workers felt racial shame about being facsimile whites. White shame, after all, was part of Frank Rissaro's problem. He felt like an intruder in his own white suburban world, and *that* white world attacked him and his children to make certain that he got the message: he was not white enough to be worthy of more respect.

By overlooking this intraracial attack going on within the white community, Sennett and Cobb are thus at a loss to explain a certain behavior pattern of these seemingly racially nondescript workers: they attack black Americans. During the late 1960s and early 1970s, these workers were the "hardhatters" who vilified the northern civil rights movement as well as the white student protest movement. The two social scientists are thus forced to use a value judgment in place of analysis that would elucidate the rationale for these attacks. They suggest that the workers chose the "wrong targets."[44] This is a woefully inadequate explanation.

I would argue that, as *white* workers, they chose to target those persons who might challenge the one "objective" modicum of prestige that they have gained through their "forced integration" into white America and that they have done so regardless of their ethnicity or class: their race is publicly "white" when compared to that of "blacks." These workers also attacked white student radicals and any other group that threatened to expose their own racial *and* class shame by challenging the rules and categories of the status quo. Like Podhoretz, they raged against those who threatened to expose their own self-deprecating, self-accusing, hidden anxieties and feelings of inner death, which are the emotional content of the workers' racial, ethnic, *and* class identities. By ignoring the racial component of the workers' "hidden" *class* and ethnic injuries, this social-scientific study perpetuated America's "dirty little [white] secret" that denies the very real link between Euro-American class and race problems.

# THREE

# CLASS

The history of white racial attacks against Euro-Americans is older than the nation and has yet to be adequately understood. The story begins in colonial America with the attempt by upper-class Virginians to control their own servants' and ex-bondsmen's behavior by giving them white racial privileges. The contempt against the lower classes entailed in the decision to elevate them racially is difficult to distinguish from the contempt that today is called racism.[1] Such a distinction is hard to make because in colonial Virginia before 1660, as social historian Edmund S. Morgan notes in his groundbreaking book *American Slavery, American Freedom: The Ordeal of Colonial Virginia*, class prejudice was difficult to distinguish from race prejudice.[2]

For purposes of our discussion, I shall use the term *classism* to refer to racial strategies devised to hide and thereby to promote or to protect economic class interests. The term *racism* will refer to racial strategies devised to hide feelings of racial shame either by diverting attention to the supposed racial flaws in others or by calling attention to oneself as racially superior.[3] The distinction between economic and psychological uses of race highlighted by these two terms will allow me to trace out how an upper-class economic ploy (classism) became a lower-class psychological need (racism).

## Colonial Virginia's Race Laws

In 1670, the Virginia assembly, consisting of some of the colony's most successful and powerful men,[4] forbade free Negroes and Indians to own Christian (that is to say, white)[5] servants. In 1676, the assembly made it legal to enslave Indians. From 1680 on, white Christians were free to give "any negroe or other slave" who dared to lift his hand in opposition to a Christian thirty lashes on the bare back. In 1705, masters were forbidden to "whip a Christian white servant naked." Nakedness was for brutes, the uncivil, the non-Christian. That same year, all property — "horses, cattle, and hogs" — was confiscated from slaves and sold by church wardens for the benefit of poor whites.[6] By means of such acts, social historian Edmund Morgan argues, the tobacco planters and ruling elite of Virginia raised the legal status of lower-class whites relative to that of Negroes and Indians, whether free, servant, or slave.

The legislators also raised the status of white servants, white workers, and the white poor in relation to their masters and other white superiors. In 1705, the assembly required masters to provide white servants at the end of their indentureship with corn, money, a gun, clothing, and — at the insistence of the English government — fifty acres of land. The poll tax was also reduced. As a result of such legal changes in the status of the white "small man's economic position," he gained legal, political, emotional, social, and financial status that was directly related to the concomitant degradation of Indians and Negroes.[7]

By means of such race laws, Virginia's ruling class systematically gave their blessing to lower-class whites, whom they nevertheless considered "the scruff and scum of England" and who now, free in the colonies after indentured servitude, were thought of as the "rabble" of Virginia.[8] What prompted the members of the ruling elite to racially elevate persons they despised? Morgan reminds us how radical these race laws were when he notes that the

> stereotypes of the poor expressed so often in England during the late seventeenth and eighteenth centuries were often identical with the descriptions of blacks expressed in colonies dependent upon slave labor, even to the extent of intimating the subhumanity of both: the [white] poor were "the vile and brutish part of mankind"; [blacks] "a brutish sort of people." In the eyes of unpoor Englishmen, the poor bore many of the marks of an alien race.[9]

Such a characterization of the poor is consistent with a meaning of *race* that at that time suggested something like what we mean by *class* today. As cultural scholar Ann Laura Stoler notes in her book *Race and the Education of Desire,* the "race" of the rising English industrial class pertained not to their color or physiognomy but to their class status, sexual and social mores, and manners, which were bourgeois.[10] Accordingly, racial superiority and thus the right to rule came to be equated with middle-class respectability and a middle-class disposition. The poor, by definition, could not belong to this new bourgeois race.

Morgan writes that some of the "alien," bedraggled, and penniless Englishmen and women were shipped to Virginia, and

> [w]hen their masters began to place people of another color in the fields beside them, the unfamiliar appearance of the newcomers may well have struck them as only skin deep. There are hints that the two despised groups initially saw each other as sharing the same predicament. It was common, for example, for servants and slaves to run away together, steal hogs together, get drunk together. It was not uncommon for them to make love together.[11]

Such intraclass collaboration took place throughout the Anglo-American colonies. In the British West Indies, for example, legislation was passed in 1701 that forbade the importation of Irish Catholics and subsequently of any Europeans to the island of Nevis because European servants had combined with African slaves to rebel against the ruling elite. A law had been passed two years earlier to forbid servants and slaves to " 'company' or to drink together."[12]

Why did the Virginian plantation masters elevate the racial status of their white servants, workers, and other "rabble"? An adequate answer to this question requires attention to the new role slavery began to play in Virginia as the seventeenth century wore on. By 1660, it had become more profitable for the "labor barons" to buy slaves rather than the service of indentured servants.[13] Accordingly, in 1660, Dutch ships, now exempted from local tax duties, began to bring more Negroes to the colony.

A host of reasons explain this shift from indentured servants to slaves, including a dwindling pool of prospects for indentured servitude and a decline in mortality from diseases in the colony, which made slaves, although twice the price of purchase of indentured servants, a better long-term investment: both they and their progeny would be in servitude for life, and the amount of time and work extracted from them would be extreme. To increase the labor produced by their slaves, the masters had only to increase the severity of pain through beatings and maimings, and to enact laws to protect themselves from prosecution for the inadvertent killings that might result. In 1669, masters exempted themselves from criminal suit for such slave slayings: predetermined malice was not assumed since no man would want "to destroy his own estate." By the end of the century, slaves made up half of Virginia's labor force.[14]

This new setup, however, required a new strategy for social control, for the natural class affinities between indentured servants and slaves presented a danger to the masters. As Edmund Morgan acidly notes, Virginia's early legislators did not have to enact slave laws to begin slavery; they simply began to purchase slaves instead of indentured English servants. As the slave population began to increase significantly, these same colonial tobacco planters, landed gentry, and English-appointed governors, however, did have to generate race laws to create animosity for the African slaves among the white servile and working classes. To this end, they legislated white race privileges for a class of persons they both despised and feared: ex-bondsmen.[15]

To understand the fear, we must note that until 1660, the majority of workers on the Virginia tobacco plantations were indentured servants, who were kept in separate servant quarters, supervised by overseers, and whipped as a means of "correction." Like their eighteenth-century slave counterparts, they were often underfed and underclothed. As indentured servants, they ran away rather than rebelling as a class.[16]

As freedmen, however, which meant "persons without house and land," they did rebel. Led by a wellborn Englishman named Nathaniel Bacon, a government official who ironically held wealthy Virginians in contempt because of their "vile" (lower-class) beginnings, the freedmen first slaughtered Indians and then turned their guns on the ruling elite. The rebels were rankled by unfair taxes, legislators' greed, and land use regulations that relegated the majority of the freedmen to the status of workers for hire rather than landowners. "Bacon's Rebellion" of 1676 did not end before Jamestown was burned to the ground. Bacon died, and the English intervened militarily. Last to surrender was a group of eighty Negroes and twenty English servants.[17]

With a swelling slave population, the masters faced the prospect of white freemen with "disappointed hopes" joining forces with slaves of "desperate hope" to mount ever more virulent rebellions. The elites' race strategy decreased the probability of such intraclass rebellions.[18] The problem of how to redirect the class interests of the "rabble" so that they would not bond with slaves was resolved through the sinister design of racism. Writes Morgan:

> The answer to the problem, obvious if unspoken and only grad-ually recognized, was racism, to separate dangerous free whites from dangerous slave blacks by a screen of racial contempt.[19]

Racial contempt would function as a wall between poor whites and blacks protecting masters and their slave-produced wealth from *both* lower-class whites and slaves. At the same time, the new laws led the poor whites to identify with the ruling elite, an identification with an objective basis in fact — otherwise this divide-and-conquer class strategy would not have worked. The Virginia assembly gave the white servant a number of class privileges associated with the elite: the right, for example, to whip a black servant or slave. These laws also gave legal protection to the poor white against the white elite by forbidding the elite to strip their white Christian servants and beat them naked.

Such laws engendered a psychological allegiance to the elite through abuse: the right to abuse those below them and a constraint on the abuse meted out by those above them. Of course, this alle-giance, and the laws that engendered it, did not protect the white servant from being beaten. The laws simply limited the abuse and thus, in the guise of a humane reform, actually continued the veiled threat of legally sanctioned violence against both the black and white servant and worker.

In addition to their marginal privileges vis-à-vis punishment, poor whites acquired new political and social advantage by means of these new laws, along with the legislated right to feel superior to all non-whites. A quota system of "deficiency laws" was established to link white workers to black slaves to ensure the equilibrium of the race-based, class status quo. Plantation owners were required by law to "employ at least one 'white' for every so many 'Negroes,' the pro-portion varying from colony to colony and time to time, from one-to twenty (Nevis, 1701) to one-to-four (Georgia, 1750)."[20] Penal laws also urged slave owners to bar Negroes from trades in order to pre-serve those positions for "white" artisans.[21] The link between white work and the condition of the black became pervasive and became bound in the mind of the white worker to a reality of and *necessity* for black slavery.

Poor whites did not, however, become economic equals with the elite. Though the economic status of both groups rose, the gap between the wealthy and poor widened as a result of slave productivity.[22] Thus, the sense that poor whites now shared status and dignity with their social betters was largely illusory.[23]

A new multiclass "white race" would emerge from the Virginia laws as one not biologically engineered but socially constructed. Its creation was determined not by genes but by gentry motivated by class interests and wanting social control.[24] The laws and the racial contempt they generated would sever ties of previous mutual interest and goodwill between European and African servants and workers, provide the ruling elite with a "buffer" of poor whites between themselves and the slaves to keep blacks down, and prevent either group from separately challenging the class interests of the elite.[25] The very definition of the white would now be legally bound to the inferior social status of the black.

Virginia's race laws thus marked the beginning of a new era during which the camaraderie among persons of different colors who found common cause because of similar social circumstances and class status gradually gave way to a racial antipathy that put an end to any interracial advance toward common class interests. And as various colonies emulated other Virginia policies, so did many of them also follow Virginia's leadership in slavery law,[26] so that not only Virginia but also the emerging nation were now on the road to establishing a legal caste system that would be based on the precept of black inferiority and white superiority. Such a system, in the words of A. Leon Higginbotham Jr., the former chief judge of the United States Court of Appeals for the Third Circuit, was designed to "*[p]resume, protect, and defend the ideal of superiority of whites and the inferiority of blacks.*"[27] We must not forget, however, that white racism was from the start a vehicle for classism; its primary goal was not to elevate a race but to denigrate a class. White racism was thus a means to an end, and the end was the defense of Virginia's class structure and the further subjugation of the poor of all "racial" colors.

Interestingly, there are records of early resistance to these race laws by the newly whited lower classes. When, for example, the Virginia assembly passed legislation in 1691 to prevent mixed marriages and thus mulatto offspring ("that abominable mixture and spurious issue"), residents petitioned the assembly in 1699 "for the Repeale of the Act of Assembly, Against English people's Marrying with Negroes Indians or Mulattoes." The petition, after internal legislative maneuvers, was ignored.[28] During this same period, an English woman named Ann Wall was arraigned by a county court and charged with "keeping company with a negro under pretense of marriage." She was convicted, bound with her two mulatto children to indentured service in another county, and told that if she ever returned to her home county of Elizabeth City, she would be banished to the Barbadoes.[29]

And, of course, there is a vast record of the escalating antipathy of the upper classes to racial mixing. Thomas Jefferson demonstrates this hostility in his own draft of race laws for Virginia, which, if accepted, would have declared any black freedman or freedwoman or any white woman who had given birth to a black or mulatto child and remained in the commonwealth for more than a year "outside the law." Such a person, under Jefferson's draft law, could be killed with impunity by anyone.[30]

At the beginning of the eighteenth century, free Negroes, although prevented from marrying whites, nevertheless, legally, still had the same labor and economic opportunities as free white servants. But, as historian John H. Russell notes in his book *The Free Negro in Virginia,* the legislature soon began stripping Negroes of these rights, and by 1723, free Negroes had lost the right to "vote, the right to bear arms, and the right to bear witness." The goal was to reinforce the recently constructed racial caste system by means of a complete and total "imposition upon the negro of a low and servile station" and, through mandated separation of the so-called races, to create an "alien race" in the midst of a white civilization.[31] By the time of the Civil War, free Negroes in Virginia would be barred from professional work as "lawyers doctors...teachers and preachers."[32]

These race laws enacted to degrade free Negroes gradually influenced both the class and racial perceptions of the "white" Virginians as the memories of shared, class-based, communal life and work with Negroes were lost with the death of the first generations of Virginians. Thus, by 1825, free white laborers refused to work next to free Negroes and either emigrated to the West or festered in extraordinary poverty because their pride of race would not permit them to associate with members of the reviled caste. For example, in 1825, citizens of Henrico County in Virginia asserted that "[w]hile [the free negro] remained here..., no white laborer will seek employment near him. Hence, it is that in some of the richest counties east of the

Blue Ridge the white population is stationary and in many others it is retrograde."[33] Noting the pattern of white emigration from Virginia, Governor Smith, in his 1847 message to the legislature, said, "I venture the opinion that a larger emigration of our white laborers is produced by our free negroes than by the institution of slavery."[34]

Poor whites' racial antipathy toward free Negro Virginians[35] resulted from the elites' classism strategies and not only staved off political collaboration but furthered the ends of white employers who preferred Negro freedmen over whites because they were cheaper to hire. Also, because the former had no legal protections, they were totally subject to their employers' wishes and whims. As Governor Smith complained in 1848, white jobs were eliminated because free Negroes "wholly supersede by the smallness and nature of their compensation the employment of white men." The governor further noted that "they perform a thousand little menial services to the exclusion of the white man, preferred by their employers because of the authority and control which they can exercise and frequently because of the ease and facility with which they can remunerate such services."[36] Classism augmented by racism thus succeeded in disempowering the white Virginia lower classes, but these whites' racism further disempowered them by distracting them from the class exploitation that they shared with Negroes.

W. E. B. Du Bois, in his seminal work, *Black Reconstruction in America: 1860–1880,* never loses sight of the fact that the true significance of slavery in the United States pertained to labor. With regard to the social development of America, Du Bois noted that the issue was one of social control and the kind of freedom that should be given to labor: black as well as white. "Was the rule of the mass of Americans to be unlimited?" This was the "great and primary question" on the minds of the framers of the Constitution, and it remained for Du Bois the open problem of democracy.[37]

As Du Bois notes, the poor white could not conceive of himself as a laborer because of labor's association with Negro toil. Rather, the poor white, if he aspired at all, aspired to become a planter and own "niggers." Accordingly, he transferred his hatred for the slave system to the Negro and by so doing stabilized the entire slave system as "overseer, slave driver and member of the patrol system. But above and beyond this role in maintaining the slave system, it fed his vanity because it associated [him] with the masters." This association with the southern elite, however, was a one-way affair. As one observer noted, "For twenty years, I do not recollect ever to have seen or heard these non-slaveholding whites referred to by the Southern gentlemen as constituting any part of what they called the South."[38]

The poor whites' vanity was thus based on both fact and illusion. The fact pertained to the poor whites' race. They *did* have the race "privilege" of not being slaves and legal rights as citizens because they were white. The illusion pertained to their class status. Their race made them think of themselves as planters and aristocrats, while their actual economic and social condition was dire. Only 25 percent of the poor whites were literate. In his 1856 book, *A Journey to the Seaboard Slave States,* Frederick L. Olmstead noted their living conditions in the following passage, which describes a backwoods settlement:

> A wretched log hut or two are the only habitations in sight. Here reside, or rather take shelter, the miserable cultivators of the ground, or a still more destitute class who make a precarious living by peddling "lightwood" in the city....
>
> These cabins ... are dens of filth. The bed if there be a bed is a layer of something in the corner that defies scenting. If the bed is nasty, what of the floor? What of the whole enclosed space? What of the creatures themselves? Pough! Water in use as a purifier is unknown. Their faces are bedaubed with the muddy accumulation of weeks. They just give them a wipe when they see a stranger to take off the blackest dirt.... The poor wretches seem startled when you address them, and answer your questions cowering like culprits.

As for poor urban whites, he wrote:

> I saw as much close packing, filth and squalor, in certain blocks inhabited by laboring whites in Charleston, as I have witnessed in any Northern town of its size; and greater evidences of brutality and ruffianly character, than I have ever happened to see, among an equal population of this class, before.[39]

Clearly, then, the poor white masses, like the black slaves, were also racial victims of the upper class. The two exploited, racialized groups differed, however, in their degree of self-awareness. The vast majority of the slaves knew they were victims of white racism, while the vast majority of poor whites did not know that they were too.

To understand the racial violence meted out to the whited lower classes by the ruling elite, we can, for example, observe the voting eligibility requirements in the South. Here we find the class conflict and contempt within the white race that the interracial conflicts were designed to obscure. As Du Bois observes, "Most Southern state governments required a property qualification for the Governor," and in South Carolina, the minimum value of his financial worth was stipulated: ten thousand pounds. "In North Carolina, a man must own 50 acres to vote for a Senator." Thus in 1828, out of 250 voters in Wilmington, North Carolina, only 48 men had the qualifications to vote for a senator.

The white southern elite also established the "extraordinary rule" of counting all or at least three-fifths of black slaves as part of the basis of representation in the legislature. This concentrated political power not only degraded, in theory, the personhood of people with African ancestry by legally counting such persons as only three-fifths human, but also in actual practice disfranchised virtually all white southerners by increasing the political presence of masters with slaves.[40] Although there were two million slaveholders in the South in 1860, an oligarchy of eight thousand actually ruled the South.[41] Simply stated, at the beginning of the Civil War, 7 percent of the total white population in the South owned almost three-quarters (three million) of all the slaves in this country.

This small planter class thus succeeded in controlling the five million whites who were too poor to own slaves, through a white class contempt that I call *white classism*. The contempt of the upper class for the lower classes resulted in the latter's contempt for any of their own class interests that exceeded their definition as whites.

## White (Class) Shame

By the time of the Civil War, poor whites were indeed white supremacists who extolled their own merit in racial rather than class terms. The psychological self-destruction entailed in this celebration of race by poor whites (to the detriment of their own class interests) takes us into the realm of lower-class white shame. The 1941 classic *The Mind of the South*, by the southern essayist and social critic W. J. Cash, gives us an intimate and detailed description of the hidden injury to the southern Euro-American's personality structure by the substitution of race definition for class interests.

Today, Cash is the second most frequently cited author in college southern culture courses (the first is C. Vann Woodward), and his book remains the subject of symposia and papers. Historians of the South both love to hate the book and hate to love it, but, nevertheless, they still do.[42] An amateur Freudian who spent most of his time living at home fighting bouts of depression, melancholia, feelings of failure, and fears of sexual impotency, Cash describes the psychological price incurred by the southern Euro-American man who defines himself as white: "a fundamental split in his psyche [resulting] from a sort of social schizophrenia."[43]

Cash argues that in the antebellum South, this split was suffered by whites at every class level and pertained to one's class self-definition. Those at the top had illusions that they were as grand and ari-tocratic as the Virginians after whom they modeled themselves. Backwater cotton planters thus imitated the Virginians in manner, dress, and comportment, but they were unable to "endow their subconscious with the aristocrat's experience, which is the aristocratic manner's essential warrant. In their inmost being they carried nearly always, I think, an uneasy sensation of inadequacy for their role."[44]

The common man also wrapped himself in class illusions that separated him from the actual experiences of his life. He actively embraced the idea that he was an aristocrat, identifying with the planter class through a glowing sense of participation in the common brotherhood of white men.[45] The "ego-warming and ego-expanding distinction between the white man and the black" elevated this common white man, Cash argues,

> to a position comparable to that of, say, the Doric knight of ancient Sparta. Not only was he not exploited directly, he was himself made by extension a member of the dominant class — was lodged solidly on a tremendous superiority, which, however much the blacks in the "big house" might sneer at him, and however much their masters might privately agree with them, he could never publicly lose. Come what might, he would always be a white man. And before that vast and capacious distinction, all others were foreshortened, dwarfed, and all but obliterated.

The grand outcome was the almost complete disappearance of economic and social forces on the part of the masses. One simply did not have to get on in this world in order to achieve security, independence, or value in one's estimation and in that of one's fellows.[46]

This delusional "vast and capacious distinction," by blinding the white poor to their own class interests, reduced the common white man's economic worth to naught. Writes Cash, "Let him be stripped of this proto-Dorian rank and he would be left naked, a man without status."[47] In effect, the emotional security lent by the hand of a fine gentleman on the common man's shoulder in a friendly greeting became a substitute for economic security. Having shifted focus from class issues to racial feelings, the common white man, in effect, had been robbed by his own racial "brothers." Such racial assaults by those who ostensibly love one most can produce feelings of white shame, masked as white pride.

Cash wisely concludes that the "Old South... was a society beset by the specters of defeat, of shame, of guilt — a society driven by the need to bolster its morale, to nerve its arm against waxing odds, to justify itself in its own eyes and in those of the world."[48] He correctly refers to these psychological specters as injuries to the self that impaired the development of a mature adult sense of self. Instead, the white self became a child-man with a purely personal (rather than personal *and* social), *puerile* attitude: someone who craved the affirmation and support his flawed social environment had not provided. He had, in effect, sustained a "narcissistic injury" to the self, which resulted in displays of grandiosity coupled with feelings of low self-esteem that came, in part, from the social fact that he was a man without economic status and thus was neither admired nor respected by his class superiors. Cash calls this grandiosity hedonistic and romantic and successfully identifies the anger-rage-violence continuum that erupts when such a self is threatened.

The grandiosity of this split self, Cash argues, is a hyper-individualism "full of the chip-on-the-shoulder; swagger and brag of a boy — [a self], in brief, of which the essence was the boast, voiced or not, on the part of every southerner that he would knock hell out of whoever dared to cross him." The corollary to this puerile display, as Cash notes, is violence, which has long been endemic to southern life. He writes that "long before the Civil War and long before hatred for the black man had begun to play any direct part in the pattern (of more than three hundred persons said to have been hanged or burned by mobs between 1840 and 1860, less than ten per cent were Negroes) the South had become peculiarly the home of lynching."[49]

Such violence is, in part, a product of shame brought on by the "common man's" own failed, racial environment. As we have seen, the constructed racial identity of the poor white is not the product of an act of love and respect by a ruling white elite, but rather is the result of upper-class race ploys for the purpose of social control. The ostensible equality among whites of various classes is thus, at best, skin deep. The absence of genuine respect for the lower-class white produces feelings of shame in the common white. This is Cash's point. To hide the injury, this self is filled with contempt for others, feelings of superiority, and an incessant need to protect an already destroyed coherent sense of self from being destroyed again.

Cash's work, however, not only describes this problem but actually exemplifies it in the following way. Cash first argues that one more factor contributes to the splitting of the white self: the white association of intimate, sentient, emotive, body-based feelings with the meaning of being a Negro. This association, Cash tells us, begins in infancy as the planter's son is suckled by a black mammy. Later, the gray old black men are the white boy's storytellers and are among the most important heroes and mentors of his boyhood, and until he passes through puberty his closest friends are black children. This companionship affects virtually the "whole body of whites, young and old, [who have] constantly before their eyes the example [and] before their ears the accent of the Negro; the relationship by the second generation at least [is] nothing less than organic. Negro entered into white man as profoundly as white man entered into Negro — subtly influencing every gesture, every word, every emotion and idea, every attitude."[50]

Following Cash's logic to its implicit but underdeveloped conclusion, the split white self consists of a mind filled with white illusions of grandeur and a body enmeshed in feelings of black intimacy. But the illusions of the mind are sanctioned by the white racial environment as real, and the feelings of the body are discarded by this same racial milieu as false. The intimate, sensual language of the white body is thought of by the "white" mind as housing "black" feelings. Talking about the Negro will thus become a way of talking about the white body's own feelings, and the distinction between the white body and the Negro will be lost. The Negro, in effect, will become an artifact of the white imagination, an object used to think about the white man's own body,[51] a figment of the white self's effort to think about the body of feelings it refuses to acknowledge.

We see this erasure of the difference between the white body and the Negro in Cash's descriptions of both Negro and white feelings as two sides of the same experience of hedonistic pleasure in the antebellum South. According to Cash, the white man, even the poor white man, lives in a world of idyllic freedom from toil — "beyond the wildest dream of the European peasant and the New England farmer wrestling with a meager soil in a bitter, unfriendly climate." He refuses to work because he despises " 'nigger work' — work that smacked of servility or work in gangs under the orders of a boss." Cash, by romanticizing the "common man's" refusal to work because of labor's association with slaves and Negroes, turns the dire plight of poor whites into a false picture of an idyllic, carefree life. Cash now describes the life of the slave the same way, using words like "happy" and "carefree." Writes Cash: "The plantation . . . [a]s we know . . . had fetched in the Negro. But the Negro is notoriously one of the world's greatest romantics and one of the world's greatest hedonists."[52]

Regarding the Negro woman, Cash enters even more deeply into this false picture of a joyful life led by persons who in reality led lives filled with suffering and exploitation. Speaking of the enslaved black woman, he writes:

> Torn from her tribal restraints and taught an easy complaisance for commercial reason, [the Negro woman] was to be had for the taking. Boys on and about the plantation inevitably learned to use her, and having acquired the habit, often continued it into manhood and even after marriage. For she was natural, and could give herself up to passion in a way impossible to wives inhibited by Puritanical training. And efforts to build up a taboo against miscegenation made little real progress.[53]

Cash has been duly criticized, of course, for such characterizations of African Americans, with critics and friends noting that Cash's perspective on the South was that of the southern white man (i.e., of a racist); that his "greatest failing was his inability to understand that the South was inevitably the history of blacks as well as whites, and of blacks and whites interacting"; and that he thus "has almost nothing to say to blacks and women."[54]

From the standpoint of my analysis, Cash's descriptions of Negroes are the black side of his characterizations of whites. He is not describing African Americans. Rather, he is talking about a figment of the white imagination that James Baldwin calls "the Negro in America [that] does not really exist except in the darkness of our minds."[55] These two images of whites and Negroes in Cash's mind are two faces of the same feeling: white class shame. Rather than confront the class injury to the white self by fellow whites and thus fully face the extent of the injury to the white body from its own community, Cash turns the embodied feelings of the white into the feelings of the Negro.

This southern version of blacking up the white body is a particularly virulent form of white minstrelsy because the white performer never puts on black grease paint. Nor is this a deliberate deception. Cash's white southern mind is so deeply severed from the feelings of his body that he doesn't even realize that he has blacked up his own body and called it the Negro.

# FOUR

# LOSS

America's nineteenth-century transition from a premodern state to an industrial giant painfully redefined what being white would mean for Euro-American wage earners. As we saw in chapter 3, in the South, the master class had used white race laws to create a white racial identity among members of the lower classes for purposes of social control. In the North, the lower classes now used black slave images to help make sense of what it would mean for them to be free industrial white workers who sold their own labor and conformed their behavior to the wishes of the highest white bidder.

The shame entailed in this interclass transaction between "white" men produced America's first national cultural institution: blackface white minstrel shows, which used racial images to "mediat[e] white men's relations with other white men."[1]

## A Pleasing Insanity

To examine this new popular-entertainment form that took the nation by storm is to catch a glimpse of the "common man" as he tried to handle the shame, loss, regret, and rage produced by his new inferiority as a free but dependent worker whose behavior must conform to the expectations of his white boss. This male worker created a minstrel stage to display these feelings as if they were not his own. Night after night he would sit in the audience with other male members of his class and watch performers who were self-announced "white" men who used grease paint and burnt cork to blacken their faces and hands, put wool on their heads and bulging eyeballs over their eyes, wore gigantic, elongated shoes with flapping heels, constructed wide, flat noses for their faces, and created carnivorously cavernous mouths with dangling lower lips.[2]

Paraded before the audiences were "aristocratic niggers" and black urban dandies with names like Zip Coon or Count Julius Caesar Mars Napoleon Sinclair Brown, who wore "skintight 'trousa-loons,' a long-tailed coat with padded shoulders, a high ruffled collar, white gloves, an eye-piece, and a long watch chain, [and like] 'Dandy Broadway Swells'... preened and pranced across the min-strel stage on their way to 'De Colored Fancy Ball' and their other continual parties."[3]

Blackface whites, some of whom were gymnasts and called them-selves Miss Lucy Long and Lubly Fan, would leap and bound about in break-down exercises performed as cross-dressers, costumed in "some tawdry old gown of loud, crude colors... whose shortness and scantness display[ed] long frilled 'panties' and No. 13 valise shoes."[4] Hips and breasts were padded to ludicrous proportion, and the men displayed gaping mouths with lips " 'as wide as all outdoors' or so large a lover could not kiss them all at once."[5]

The performers used tambourine, fiddle, banjo, and bones ("clackers") to accompany their ragtag dress and antics as happy, sentimental, festive plantation slaves, pickanninies, mammies, un-cles, aunts, and sambos in productions like *The Sports and Pastimes of the Virginia Colored Race,* portraying slaves who spent their days like carefree children bursting forth in songs with lyrics such as "Nigga's hearts am bery gay / Dey tink ob nothin but to play," as they looked forward to the arrival of their benevolent master, who "comes to see our sports... '[c]ause de merriment of niggers often makes him laugh."[6]

The playbills for the shows "continually featured paired pictures of the performers in blackface and without makeup — rough and respectable, black and white."[7] The audience was also repeatedly reminded of its whiteness with songs that began with the words, "Now, white folks... " The Euro-American blackface entertainers were, in fact, the first performers in the world to present themselves on stage as persons who were self-consciously *white.*[8]

White minstrelsy, as social historian Robert C. Toll notes in his book *Blacking Up: The Minstrel Show in Nineteenth-Century Amer-ica,* was older than the nation and until 1812 basically consisted of stock characterizations of comedic buffoons and romanticized noble savages, but now with its new stock of urban dandies and merry slaves its birthplace as America's first national, popular en-tertainment form was none other than New York City. In February

1843, the Virginia Minstrels, four blackfaced Euro-American men, performed an entire evening of the "oddities, peculiarities, eccentricities, and commicalities of that Sable Genus of Humanity." They were an instant success and by the end of the year had left for a successful English tour.[9]

Chronicling this new cultural form that swept the nation, Toll observes that in 1844,

> [o]nly a year after the first minstrel show, the Ethiopian Serenaders, a blackface minstrel troupe, played at the White House for the "Especial Amusement of the President of the United States, His Family and Friends." In subsequent years, minstrels entertained Presidents Tyler, Fillmore, and Pierce..., as well as countless common Americans throughout the nation. In response to the seemingly insatiable public demand, innumerable minstrel troupes appeared. It is impossible to determine how many there were, even in the first decade of minstrelsy, partially because of inadequate records but also because amateur and amateurish troupes appeared almost everywhere, usually only for short runs. When large numbers of people trekked across the continent in search of California gold, for example, minstrelsy by 1855 claimed five professional troupes in San Francisco alone.... Similar developments occurred wherever people were concentrated and transportation was available, especially along the Mississippi River, the rapidly expanding rail lines into the Northwest, and in the burgeoning cities of the Northeast.[10]

Within a decade, white minstrel shows had their own basic three-part format with the entire company first on stage in a semicircle with a standard fare of jokes and comic and "serious" songs and dances. Part 2 was the olio, or variety section, of miscellaneous songs, dances, acrobatics, and musical sounds made by playing such "instruments" as combs, porcupine quills, glasses, and other novelties. The third act was usually a one-act skit, which before the mid-1850s was invariably set on a plantation with the entire troupe in southern "darky" costumes.[11] The formats varied over the next fifty years but always had a give-and-take with the audience as a central attraction because minstrelsy audiences knew what they wanted, demanded it, and got it: reassurance, catharsis, and exacting interchanges that reaffirmed the men in the audience as persons who could manage and control the vital interests of their own lives. In a word, they could be powerful men. As Toll notes:

> The antebellum minstrel show, which enjoyed its greatest popularity in the Northeastern cities, drew audiences that were, if anything, more demonstrative than other theater audiences of the period. When they were pleased, they roared for encores and, at times, even threw money. When they were mildly displeased they disrupted performances with hisses and shouts. But when they felt cheated, they could become violent. They mobbed inferior troupes that had passed themselves off as famous companies and then presented third-rate shows. They also drove poor or unpopular performers from the stage with barrages of anything they could find to throw including rocks and nails.[12]

Not surprisingly, the audiences were so caught up in these performances that their fervor for them swept the country with a force that the *New York Tribune* in 1855 called a pleasing "insanity."[13]

Before the 1850s, the audiences for these shows had not yet become a self-segregated unit with their own theaters. The standard entertainment fare included minstrel acts but had something for every level of taste. The audiences were tiered by class. The boxes held socialites and would-be socialites, who "paraded their newest fashions and hair styles [and] complained that 'there was too much light on the stage and too little in the boxes' so that it was difficult to 'recognize a friend across the house.'" The lower classes sat in the gallery and the pit, below the boxes. Toll graphically depicts the scene of women nursing their babies and men spitting tobacco juice on the floor, telling jokes, cracking peanuts, eating lunches, drinking liquor, stamping their feet in time to the music, singing along, and sporadically hollering back and forth to each other.[14]

The 1849 Astor Place Riot in New York City forced the class tensions and conflicts exhibited in this heterogeneous scene to a head. Lower-class theatergoers, who despised the class elitism and effrontery of "arrogant" English actors and their loyal bourgeois American audiences, first pelted the English tragedian Charles Macready with rotten eggs, vegetables, and chairs and then rioted when prominent New Yorkers such as Washington Irving and Herman Melville persuaded the actor not to return to England but to complete his New York theatrical run. The rioters had "invoked the name of nationalism" in their misbegotten attempt to defend the honor of the American actor Edwin Forrest, with whom Macready carried on a "running battle for audiences, acclaim, and status."[15] When some of the demonstrators who gathered for the next performance by Macready were arrested by police and soldiers, a full-fledged riot erupted with troops firing on the mob, killing thirty-one rioters and spectators, and injuring 150 civilians, policemen, and soldiers.[16]

This event, as Toll notes in describing it, was unlike the numerous major riots in antebellum American cities because this was a class conflict rather than a riot against various minority scapegoats such as Catholics, abolitionists, and blacks. With this event, a social taboo had been broken. As the *Philadelphia Ledger* noted, "There is now in our country what every good patriot has hitherto considered it his duty to deny — a high class and a low class."[17]

Unadorned classism was now on display: class conflict revealed as an intraracial issue between whites. Class tensions, resentment, and grievances within the same "race" could no longer be deflected by an interracial, scapegoating ploy. The work of social historians Herbert G. Gutman and Ira Berlin brings both the class and the race issues within the so-called white race into bold relief by uncovering what other Euro-American historians failed to notice: the racial as well as class diversity hidden by a blanket use of the term *white*.

## Before Whiteness

Until recently, as Gutman and Berlin note in their essay "Class Composition and the Development of the American Working Class, 1840–1890," American historians assumed that most nineteenth-century wage earners were native-born whites; that a native-born white working class had emerged before 1840 and had reproduced itself; and that immigrants, their children, and others were outside the mainstream American history of labor.[18] Each of these assumptions, as Gutman and Berlin carefully demonstrate, is wrong.

Historians made these errors because they failed to note that the formation and subsequent development of an American working class comprised two distinct but overlapping stages. The first stage began during the American Revolution and ended during the 1840s.

The second stage developed between 1840 and World War I. Historians thus overlooked the fact that, whereas the workers in the first stage were native-born Euro-Americans, the American workers shaped by the second stage were immigrants or the children of immigrants.

In fact, using statistical analysis Gutman and Berlin show that not less than three-quarters of the American wage-earning workers after 1840 were indeed immigrants or the children of immigrants.[19] These two historians thereby opened a historical window on a race war about class identity within white America. Previous historians had made the labor conflicts within this period seem enigmatic and the conflicts between popular and elite culture that were produced by and expressive of these events difficult to decipher.[20] Gutman and Berlin challenged the unquestioned assumption of an undifferentiated white American mass and thus presented a revisionist white social history, that is, a study of white American nineteenth-century workers as a neglected group. Such a history, as another social historian, George P. Rawick, trenchantly noted, would have to address race and class conflicts within racialized groups as well as between them. By avoiding such material, Rawick concludes, historians have written "very little . . . social history of the American people."[21]

In focusing on such conflicts, the historian of nineteenth-century industrializing America must note that the premodern cultures and work habits of the men and women who became factory workers in *both* stages of labor development were "ill fitted to the regular routines demanded by machine-centered factory processes."[22] As Herbert Gutman demonstrates in graphic detail in his book *Work, Culture, and Society in Industrializing America,* the work habits required of these new workers seemed both strange and useless to them and, thus, from the manufacturers' perspective, produced irregular and undisciplined behavior among their workers that lowered their profits. As Gutman reminds us, in 1860, there were more slaves than industrial workers in America and the value of American products ranked behind the value of those of England, Germany, or France. Thirty-four years later, the value of American products was almost as much as the value of the products of these three countries combined. Clearly American manufacturers had successfully designed rules to break their new workers of the preindustrial behavior patterns. Textile factory work rules are a case in point. Gutman notes:

A New Hampshire cotton factory that hired mostly women and children forbade "spiritous liquor, smoking, [or] any kind of amusement...in the workshops, yards, or factories" and promised the "immediate and disgraceful dismissal" of employees found gambling, drinking, or committing "any other debaucheries." A Massachusetts firm nearby insisted that young workers unwilling to attend church stay "within doors and improve their time in reading, writing, and in other valuable and harmless employment." Tardy and absent Philadelphia workers paid fines and could not "carry into the factory nuts, fruits, etc.; books, or paper." A Connecticut textile mill owner justified the twelve-hour day and the six-day week because it kept "workmen and children" from "vicious amusements." He forbade "gaming...in any private house."

As in colonial Virginia, lower-class men were again a special problem for the "owning classes." As the owner of a Massachusetts woolen mill observed, his business required "more man labour," but he avoided it because "[w]omen are much more ready to follow good regulations, are not captious, and do not clan as the men do against the overseers." Male factory workers in Medford, Massachusetts, for example, quit when they were refused grog privileges. Among Philadelphia ironworkers, absenteeism was rampant at the rural Hopewell Village forge: "hunting, harvesting, wedding parties, frequent 'frolicking' that sometimes lasted for days, and uproarious Election and Independence Day celebrations plagued the mill operators." In the diary of one New Jersey iron manufacturer were such entries as "all hands drunk"; "molders all agree to quit work and went to the beach"; "Peter Cox very drunk and gone to bed"; and "Edward Rutter off a-drinking." One woman who worked in a New England factory before the Civil War recalled that her employer first hired "all American girls," but later hired immigrant laborers because "not coming from country homes, but living as the Irish do, in the town, they take no vacations, and can be relied on at the mill all year round."[23]

Such behavior was typical of first-generation factory workers, native- or foreign-born. That work must be routinized, performed without regard to one's mood, and kept discrete from one's personal interests, separated from one's family life and values, was alien to preindustrial agrarian and peasant folk. They thus had to learn to separate work from pleasure, means from ends, life values and wage envelope. The later immigrant workers were constantly disciplined and reprimanded for their lazy, idle, nonproductive, and mindless ways, as had been the first-generation, native-Euro-American factory workers. And later generations of native workers, when they subsequently became the urban Euro-American population of America's expanding metropolitan centers of industry, "scarcely remembered that native Americans had once been hesitant first-generation factory workers."[24] Instead, they sneered at the behavior and work habits of each new wave of immigrants who became America's new industrial workers. What happened to these native-born workers' memories? Why were these ordeals forgotten? Where did the memories of them go?

This scarcity of memory is all the more intriguing because the premodern cultural patterns and "tenacious" premodern work habits of these newly industrialized workers were not entirely shattered by the manufacturers' constant attempts to transform them into highly regulated, disciplined industrial workers. Preindustrial men who had full control of their work hours as farmers, artisans, and peasants held on to the tradition of eruptions of idleness in the midst of labor that had defined their former work lives.[25] Accordingly, self-imposed relaxation periods for morning and afternoon sweet cookies, cakes, and candies sold by vendors that broke up the artisans' work day in New York City shipyards became a custom as necessary as a grindstone.[26]

Such work habits persisted in each new generation of industrial workers, first in the native-born Euro-Americans and then in the immigrant workers and their children. This resistance to modernizing technology, which eventually displaced the premodern work habits and patterns, also gave continuity to the era through an overlap of interests between the first industrial workers and their immigrant heirs.[27] Neither the profound economic changes underway as this country geared up to become an industrial giant nor the Civil War demolished the retention of premodern artisan work habits. Gutman is adamant on this point. His work is pathfinding, in part, because of the primary historical data he discovered through his systematic study of the newspapers and other documents of the era, overlooked by other historians, which made this point self-evident. Although suffering and poverty cut deeply into this new working-class world, restructuring the everyday texture of these new industrial workers' lives, and although "there is no reason to neglect or idealize such suffering,... it is time to discard the notion that the large-scale uprooting and exploitative processes that accompanied industrialization caused little more than cultural breakdown and social anomie. Family, class, and ethnic ties did not dissolve easily."[28] Thriving immigrant, ethnic subcultures held on to preindustrial traditions. These traditions differed from the industrial workers' new "white" identities, which pertained to values associated with the necessity of being an efficient worker. The ethnic traditions had to do with family concerns and the festivities, rituals, and celebrations of life associated with networks of voluntary human relationships:

> A model subculture included friendly and benevolent societies as well as friendly local politicians, community-wide holiday celebrations, an occasional library..., participant sports, churches sometimes headed by a sympathetic clergy, saloons, beer gardens, and concert halls or music halls and, depending upon circumstances, trade unionists, labor reformers, and radicals.[29]

The groups varied depending upon ethnic makeup, class, and occupational distinctions. Writes Gutman:

> As late as 1888, residents in some Rhode Island mill villages figured their wages in British currency. Common rituals and festivals bound together such communities. Paterson [New Jersey] silk weavers had their Macclesfield wakes, and Fall River cotton mill workers their Ashton wakes. British immigrants "banded together to uphold the popular culture of the homeland" and celebrated saints' days.... Mythic beliefs also cemented ethnic and class solidarities. The Irish-American press, for example, gave Martin O'Brennan much space to argue that Celtic had been spoken in the Garden of Eden, and in Paterson Irish-born silk, cotton, and iron workers believed in the magical powers of that town's "Dublin Spring."[30]

Immigrant, preindustrial values also went into minstrelsy. Irish minstrel performers, for example, sang Irish songs, protested anti-Irish discrimination, and celebrated Irish accomplishments — in blackface. Traditional, nonurban values were also affirmed in the 1850s, as minstrels protested dire urban living conditions and the immorality of urban dilettantes; in the 1860s they warned against new arrivals falling prey to "city slickers"; and in the 1870s and 1880s they attacked the wide disparities in wealth[31] — in blackface. Throughout this era, however, northern Negroes were steadfastly characterized as the "living embodiments of vice and folly at their most absurd."[32] Why?

One answer to the vilification of northern African Americans certainly must pertain to classism: the way in which white workers learned to think of black workers as an economic threat. The extent of the link between white workers' condition and the social condition of black men and women is vividly shown by the reasoning of the white defenders of the Columbia, Pennsylvania, race riot of 1834. The white rioters used the Declaration of Independence as the basis of their appeal, charging that there was a plot between their employers and abolitionists to open new trades to black men and thus "break down the distinctive barrier between the colors that the poor whites may gradually sink into the degraded condition of the Negroes — that like them, they may be slaves and tools."[33] Regarding this plea, historian David Roediger notes:

> Though the animus was ostensibly directly toward the weak Blacks and their designing manipulators, the fear that any change in the status of Blacks could show white freedom to be illusory runs through the document, and "colored freeholders" were singled out for removal from the borough.[34]

But something more than classism was underway on stage. To get at its basis in both race and class, we must take note of the nature and extent of the attacks by white industrialists and other members of the white middle class against the immigrant workers. Gutman, in his book *Work, Culture, and Society in Industrial America*, presents a list of some of the invectives hurled at the immigrant workers:

- In 1859, the Jersey City *American Standard* called Irishmen who caused disorder as they sought wages due them from the Erie Railroad "animals" and "a mongrel mass of ignorance and crime and superstition, as utterly unfit for its dues, as they are for the common courtesies and decencies of civilized life."

- In 1869, *Scientific American* told the "ruder" laborers of Europe who were welcomed to American shores that if they did

not "assimilate" quickly, they would face a "quiet but sure extermination." They must change their ways or "share the fate
of the native Indian."

- In the mid-1870s, the Chicago *Post-Mail* characterized its city's
  Bohemian population as "depraved beasts, harpies, decayed
  physically and spiritually, mentally and morally, thievish and
  licentious." The Chicago *Tribune* called striking immigrant
  brickmakers men but "not reasoning creatures."

- During this same time period, the Chicago *Times* complained
  that the country had become "the cess-pool of Europe under
  the pretense that it is the asylum of the poor." It characterized
  the city's Slavic inhabitants as descendants of Scythians, "eaters
  of raw animal food, fond of drinking the blood of their enemies
  whom they slew in battle, and [men] who preserved as trophies
  the scalps and skins of enemies whom they overthrew." And
  again there was talk of extermination: "Let us whip these slavic
  wolves back to the European dens from which they issue, or
  in some way exterminate them." The *New York Times* would
  echo similar sentiments fifteen years later.[35]

A demand for complete and immediate assimilation by European
immigrants, and the veiled or direct threat of annihilation for those
who failed to do so, produced a "destruction of memories" that
seemed to one commentator akin to the fervid demand by the church
fathers for a confession of sin as "sudden, complete, and bitter."[36]
To protest this demand, W. I. Thomas in his 1921 book, *Old World
Traits Transplanted,* made a racial plea tied to the common interests of a common white race. Thomas acknowledges, for example,
that it is impossible to think calmly about the prospect of "the
white race as dying out"[37] but seeks to demonstrate that the European immigrants, unlike the "coolies" and Africans, do not pose
such a threat. To make his racial point, he recounts a story related by Dr. David Livingston of two African men who laughed at
a child whose body had been disfigured by illness. These Africans,
Thomas argues,

> could not appreciate the painting of a Madonna because they
> have not developed our tenderness toward children, because
> white men and women impress them somewhat as cadavers and

albinos impress us..., because they have not our tradition of
chivalry and know nothing of the sufferings of our Lord.

Between European immigrants and Americans, in contrast, there is,
Thomas continues, a "certain identity of experiences and memories
...of main importance for assimilation." Thomas thus pleads for
white Americans to stop the assault on their white European racial
kin. It is shortsighted, he writes, to force European immigrants to
give up their traditional identities as if they bring nothing "of value
for the future in the whole of past experience."[38]

Thomas, of course, was correct to see the white racial contempt
against immigrant workers and their offspring in their treatment and
depictions by Euro-Americans. Talk of animality, lack of civilized
ways, and extermination had the taint of racial hatred. The negative
evaluation of their worth, however, was based on social habits, behavior, and temperament. The immigrants were told that they would
have to become "sober, orderly and moral" workers.[39]

This was a period of transition, and the workers had to relearn
what was deemed appropriate and inappropriate behavior not only
for the workplace but also for their lives in general. The "destruction
of memory" referred to by Thomas is an apt way of thinking about
both the socialization and assimilation processes for native-born
and immigrant premodern workers who had to become industrial
workers in order to survive.

The workers during the second half of the nineteenth century became the "transitional" group, the workers who could still recall
what they were being required to forget in order to "make it" in industrializing America. A collective amnesia had not yet set in. They
had not yet been completely cut off from their past because they
themselves were the link between the passing old order and the coming new order of things. As Gutman notes, the workers, unlike their
twentieth-century progeny, had not yet been

> deprived of access to the historical processes that had shaped
> their lives, the lives of their parents, and the nation at large.
> This amnesia was not peculiar to one or another region. It
> happened throughout the entire nation between 1910 and
> 1940, decades during which the Progressive synthesis framed
> the writing of American history, but during which mainstream
> American culture increasingly celebrated "American-ness" by

defining it narrowly and identifying it with achievement and assimilation.[40]

As a transitional group between the old and the new, the premodern and the modern, the disorderly industrial worker and the orderly industrial peasant, farmer, or villager, these workers were forced to mediate contending claims made upon them by their traditions and their emerging self-definitions. They had to face what they must lose and what they must acquire. The economic success achieved by one immigrant led him to say, "I have been successful. I have property. My children have superior advantages. But *I have lost my life.*" As Thomas notes in commenting upon this statement, the immigrant's loss pertained to the "memories of his home conditions, of leisure and festivities, of joys and sorrows shared by an intimate group." For the first-generation immigrant, Thomas concludes, his success can never be complete because he knows what he has lost cannot be recouped: himself in his preimmigrant world of values as a valued member of his own community.[41]

These immigrant memories were not about selves held in high regard because they and their communities were white. These remembered self-identities were not white: they were Irish, Italian, Slavic, German, English, Catholic, Jewish, Russian....Their colors were olive, sallow, and peaches and cream. Their religious values affirmed a world of relationships that could not be reduced to commercial interests and gain. Assimilation, Thomas suggested, "may be compared with skin grafting, where the new tissue is not applied to the whole surface, but spots are grafted, and from these the connective tissues ramify."[42]

Black grease paint covered the parts of the new industrial self that had not yet been covered by this racial skin grafting. The process of forgetting their prewhited selves began to empty the workers' core sense of self and of values that transcended the workplace and its behavior-modification requirements. The premodern and its desires had to be thought of as loathsome, and thus had to be suppressed. These strangulated desires are where the premodern Euro-American and immigrant met the "black," who was permanently locked out of modern America as a thing to be despised. The hateful met the hated. The premodern feelings of "whites" married the premodern image ("Negroes") of these feelings. Both the Euro-American worker and the immigrant worker thus found an image for the self their

bosses loathed but the workers still loved: the self that would not
fit into the routinized life it loathed but instead got drunk, went fish-
ing, took relaxation breaks, and resisted its demise as best it could.
Their attachment to the black image was a desire to recover feelings
that for themselves as "whites" were intolerable, but as prewhites
were the hallmarks of their humanity: sensuality, sexuality, free play,
the premodern home, whimsy, strutting, zipping, dashing, clowning,
cooing, cooning.

The blackface on this whited body was thus the industrial
worker's attempt to hide what he loved: his former life, earlier
feelings that he now had to learn to set aside as loathsome. This
newly whited worker hid these feelings expressive of his former life
by a mask of disgust. This is a shame strategy. Shame, as psychoanalytic theorist Susan Miller reminds us, can be conceived of as
an act of self-protection by someone whose core sense of self is repeatedly attacked. "Such shame experiences might be described as
efforts to hide the self in order to save it from further narcissistic
trauma."[43] There is strong irony here, for if we take this view of
shame, blackfaced whited men were pretending to be who they actually thought they were if their uncomfortable skin-grafting whiteness
was removed. These new workers were the other niggers: the pale
ones. They were the ones who had pale skins but were described by
their bosses as savages.

## Pale Niggers

To be sure, white minstrel shows were political forums against civil
rights for black "niggers," slave or free. Proslavery sentiment (classism) and white supremacist politics (racism) went hand in hand
on stage. Slaves were depicted as contented and their masters as
paternal. When political stakes were high, however, as abolitionist
sentiment rose in the North, the attacks became blunter and more
direct, with verbal attacks against the emancipation of the slaves,
the use of black troops in northern armies, taxation to pay for the
post–Civil War black reconstruction strategies of the Freedmen's Bu-
reau, and any government policy that seemed to favor "the nigger."[44]
When, for example, *Uncle Tom's Cabin* became a popular antislav-
ery treatise, "minstrels replied with proslavery versions, featuring
tunes like 'Happy Are We, Darkies So Gay.'"

David Toll makes this point forcefully in his survey of nineteenth-century white blackface minstrelsy, observing that "[e]ven sympathetic black characters were cast as inferiors. Minstrels used heavy dialect to portray Negroes as foolish, stupid and compulsively musical." No heroic white characters were needed to make the point. White superiority was established through negation: the ceaseless and pervasive degradation of the black. Abolitionist and ex-slave Frederick Douglass referred to the lot of these performers as "the filthy scum of white society, who had stolen from us a complexion denied to them by nature, in which to make money, and pander to the corrupt taste of their white fellow citizens."[45] From this standpoint, white minstrelsy was "half a century of inurement to the uses of white supremacy."[46]

What is not self-evident, however, is the racial contempt of and protest by these Euro-American and immigrant men against their own white racial identities. *Higher-class whites* had called them vile, lazy, idle, animals, humans without reasoning capacity. *They* had been threatened with extermination like the "native Indian" by one of white America's most respectable newspapers if they did not become white. *They* had been beaten and jailed by the armed police forces and private patrol forces of the white state when they rampaged against white elite tastes and snobbery, or when they struck or tried to unionize. *They* had been told to go to church, to control their sexual desires, to work long shifts for their own moral uplift. To understand the class contempt experienced by these men because of who *they* were is to begin to take the formation of a white identity seriously as a process rather than as a finished fact. Such a perspective requires the observer to acknowledge that there was indeed a nonwhite self before their new white racial and class identities were formed.

It is appropriate that both David Toll and Eric Lott, two major contemporary scholars of nineteenth-century white minstrelsy whose work has greatly informed both my descriptions of and insights into white minstrelsy, would turn to psychological language to help explain the rush of feeling the performers released in their audiences. The release, if only momentarily, did indeed serve a therapeutic role. As Freud wisely suggested, people suffer because of "strangulated affects": undischarged feelings that have become intolerable to express or whose expression requires more courage than the person can muster.[47] White minstrelsy was a discharge of feeling for the audience and in this way served a psychotherapeutic function. "Psychoanalysis," as one contemporary theorist notes, "whatever else we may wish to define it as, is the systematic attempt to help people discover and get back in touch with what they feel."[48]

Toll and Lott, however, by relying on classic Freudian psycho-analytic theory, cannot adequately explain the feelings of shame entailed in the production of white minstrelsy. By focusing their analyses, respectively, on the socialization process and on homoeroticism, they miss the underlying problem of white shame.

Eric Lott, using Freudian psychology, argues that the blackfaced male bodies draped in women's clothes during an era in which women now had roles in legitimate theater fulfilled homoerotic desires: the white man's desire. Minstrel shows, Lott argues, had purposes that allowed for "something besides racism onto the American stage." A separate stage was hardly needed for racism in antebellum America, Lott reasons. The preoccupation beyond racism, Lott concludes, was with sexuality and more precisely homosexuality by way of envy of black male genitalia.[49]

Drawing on a plethora of images of the "nigger's big feet" and "astonishing" nose size, and commandeering Freud on smut to argue that the audiences wanted the black object of desire, Lott suggests that

> regardless of the attempts to demystify black men's sexuality, if not indeed amidst [these attempts], white male desire for black men was everywhere to be found in minstrel acts. Of course there was very little attempt generally to disguise the fact that uncontrollable black desire was one of the minstrel show's chief attractions whether in lubricious dances, jokes, gestures, or lyrics.

Lott suggests that "homosexual moments" that began to appear in 1840s songs allowed men to image same-sex desire. One such song is this:

> Oh, Sally is de gal for me,
> I wouldn't hab no udder,
> If Sal dies to-morrow night,
> I'll marry Sally's brudder.

The black man's sexuality, Lott argues, was "an attractive masculinity" that could mediate white men's relationship with other white men and give them a moment's reprieve so that they might return to their state of arrested adolescence at the onset of puberty.[50]

Lott, in his psychological analysis of black male images in the mind of the white male, reduces a complex civil war raging within the Euro-American man's core sense of himself to a homoerotic desire. Lott's strategy is both understandable and regrettable. Lott says that he is "after some sense of how precariously nineteenth-century white working people lived their whiteness," but he is stymied at the very beginning of his project because he assumes that the men he is studying are already white. Actually, these men — both the native-born and the immigrants — were in the process of being "whited." The actors on the minstrel stage, we must remember, had to help these men quite literally come to terms with their new racial identity by constantly reminding them that they were "white folk." Lott attempts to support his argument by reflecting upon the personal reminiscences of white men about their pubescent use of black images. As Lott notes:

In *North Toward Home...,* white Mississippian Willie Morris remembers "a stage, when we were about thirteen, in which we 'went Negro.' We tried to broaden our accents to sound like Negroes, as if there were not enough similarity already. We consciously walked like young Negroes, mocking their swinging gait, moving our arms the way they did, cracking our knuckles and whistling between our teeth." ... I would maintain that this dynamic, persisting into adulthood, is so much a part of most American white men's equipment for living that they remain entirely unaware of their participation in it. The special achievement of minstrel performers was to have intuited and formalized the white male fascination with the turn to black, which Leslie Fiedler describes this way: "Born theoretically white, we are permitted to pass our childhood as imaginary Indians, our adolescence as imaginary Negroes, and only then are expected to settle down to being what we really are: white once more." ... These common white associations of black maleness with the onset of pubescent sexuality indicate that the assumption of dominant codes of masculinity in the United States was (and still is) partly negotiated through an imaginary black interlocutor.[51]

It is self-evident in these examples used by Lott that black male images have been used to help Euro-American boys negotiate their emerging sexual identities. But Lott never reveals the mechanism by which these negotiations take place: shame. The boys feel the sexual rush of their own feelings that seek consummation through sexual association with others. All such associations, however, must be severely circumscribed in order to fit into the strictures of whiteness. The black male image thus gives the boys a way to express their own feelings without having to acknowledge their source. The black images express the boys' own "shameful" (and therefore, black) desires as they struggle to hold on to their own (denied) feelings and (fettered) desires in unfettered ways. Their imitation of "Negroes" is thus an attempt to participate freely in (their own) feelings that are beyond the pale of appropriate desire. Their apparent desire for black penises is actually the boys' own attempt to both represent and hold on to their own forbidden desires.

We found a similarly complex sexual scenario in Norman Podhoretz's reminiscences of his feelings of envy toward the Negro boys in his neighborhood. Podhoretz, we must remember, was already in the process of setting aside his own virulent, embodied feelings in order to make it in a WASP world that despised him as a Jewish male. The Negro boys in his Brooklyn neighborhood thus became "the very embodiment of the values of the street that he had abandoned: free, independent, reckless, brave, masculine, erotic." They were "beautifully, enviably tough, not giving a damn for anyone or anything" — all the things that Podhoretz dared not feel: the perilous tug toward greater freedom from WASP rules. His feelings of envy mingled with his "tears of rage" toward the Negro boys and his own "self-contempt."[52]

We also found examples of this complex, white male, imaginative longing for black male sexuality in W. J. Cash's *The Mind of the South*. Cash describes the emotional mingling that went on between the African American and Euro-American child *before* personal white racial definitions came to the fore. This mingling, Cash suggests, is "nothing less than organic." Cash's "Negro," as we saw, was actually the spitting image of the romantic, hedonistic "common white." The collapse of the very real difference between the black image in the white mind and the actual reality of the person who is thought of as "black" turned the person observed into a "Negro," an object created by the white imagination to think about its own lynched feelings of desire. This elimination of difference prevented Cash from expanding his white horizons beyond the limits of his own racial romance with whiteness.

An adequate analysis of this whitening process of the Euro-American male requires the researcher to identify the self that is not "theoretically white." This nonwhite core of the self is filled with memories of encounters with others that exceed the racial strictures of whiteness. Such experiences, for these nineteenth-century industrial workers, entailed a series of struggles to both lose and hold on to their own nonracial identities as they made the painful transition from premodern to modern workers. This struggle produced white minstrelsy as a desperate attempt to mask feelings of white shame.

The commercial movie *A Family Thing* gives us a vivid way to think about this struggle of the white male self with its own non-white core. In this movie, a white, southern bigot discovers, as an adult, that his biological mother was black. Until this discovery, this middle-aged man believed that both of his parents were white. But now he knows that his father raped the black maid. He was the baby produced by this rape and was subsequently raised by his father and his father's white wife as their own son. Upon learning of his black genealogy, the devastated redneck immediately looks at his image in a mirror and says — "nigger." White shame is the feeling that something about the self is racially beyond the pale.

What is actually beyond the pale, however, is not the discovery of a drop of black blood in one's veins. Rather, the darkness revealed within the white self is a realm of feelings of dismay, distress, loss, rage, and anger at one's own white environment because it prevented the self from retaining a fuller and more inclusive range of its own sentient feelings. This loss of feeling turns Euro-Americans into racial victims of their own white communities because their own "innards" begin to feel like the painful minstrel grimace of a pale nigger. This painful core sense of self is transmitted from one generation to the next because the child learns to wince when confronted with its own sentient, nonwhite core sense of self. Feeling black, it covers itself in shame.

David Toll also turns to psychology to help explain the function of the minstrel show in the unconscious life of the "white American common man," and, like Lott, he finds a puerile element. For Toll, however, the issue is not sexuality but socialization:

In the same informal and even unconscious ways that basic social and cultural values are transmitted to children, minstrels
communicated their implicit messages to their audiences as part
of their performance.... From the beginning, minstrels helped
audiences cope with their concerns, frustrations, and anxieties.
Lambasting aristocrats, and making extensive use of frontier
language and lore, minstrels asserted the worth and dignity of
the white American common man.

The performers did more than simply reflect the audiences' ideas and
desires — they created concrete images of them.[53]

I agree that these images were indeed created to express that
which the audiences felt but did not know how to say. An adequate
understanding of the psychological forces at play in the creation of
images that depicted these unvoiced feelings, however, requires me
to return to talk about shame. More precisely, white shame: the necessity of concealing one's own true feelings from view lest they be
racially attacked by whites — again.

# FIVE

# VICTIMS

The price of admission to the white race in America has been exacting. Costs, as we have seen in the previous chapters, have included ethnic conflicts, class exploitation, police intimidation, humiliation by teachers, child abuse, lost self-esteem, and a general feeling of self-contempt. I call these costs the wages *for* whiteness. To tally them is to give an account of a racial victim, someone who had to become white in order to survive. The story of this racial victim is rarely told.

It is much more common to speak of the benefits accorded someone for being white in America. Following the lead of W. E. B. Du Bois, I call such rewards the wages *of* whiteness. To tell this tale is to talk about privilege.[1] In the past, the wages of whiteness were considerable. Du Bois, in his book *Black Reconstruction in America: 1860–1880*, summarizes them: "public deference and titles of courtesy"; access to "public functions, public parks and the best schools"; jobs as policemen; the right to sit on juries; voting rights; flattery from newspapers while Negro news was "almost utterly ignored except in crime and ridicule."[2]

These privileges also included the right, based on legal indifference and social approval, to taunt, police, humiliate, mob, rape, lynch, jibe, rob, jail, mutilate, and burn Negroes, which became a sporting game, "a sort of permissible Roman holiday for the entertainment of vicious whites." During the late 1800s, for example, "[p]ractically all white southern men went armed and the South reached the extraordinary distinction of being the only modern civilized country where human beings were publicly burned alive."[3]

The price exacted for these privileges, however, was also considerable. Du Bois summarizes the cost in the nineteenth-century antebellum South: no major labor movements to protect the region's five million poor whites, who owned no slaves, from the eight thousand largest slaveholders, who, in effect, ruled the South. Hatred of the Negro, slave and free, blocked furtive attempts by the lower classes to fight their own race's class exploiters.[4]

Poor whites often voted with their feet by leaving the South. "In 1860, 399,700 Virginians were living out of their native state. From Tennessee, 344,765 emigrated; from North Carolina, 272,606 and from South Carolina, 256,868."[5] They settled in the Middle West and northeastern states and had a "vivid fear of the Negro as a competitor in labor, whether slave or free" because they knew that Negro laborers could always be hired for less. By playing the labor costs of both whites and Negroes against each other, contractors kept the earnings of both groups low.[6]

White privileges functioned in this downward-spiraling labor contest as a kind of "public and psychological wage" to supplement a low-paying job that could be easily lost to a lower-paid worker — before and after the Civil War.[7] All "whites" — regardless of class position — benefited from this race wage, as legal scholar Cheryl I. Harris reminds us in her essay "Whiteness as Property." For poorer wage earners "without power, money or influence," however, this wage of whiteness functioned as a kind of workers' "compensation."[8] It was a "consolation prize" to persons who, although not wealthy, would not be counted as losers because they were, at least, white.[9]

Or so it seems. These low-paid wage earners were not held in high esteem by their own white bosses, who exploited their labor while consoling them as whites. The workers were, in effect, exploited twice: both as workers and as "whites." Their "race" was used to distract them from their diminishing value as wage earners. Diminished as workers, they felt shame.[10] Inflated as whites, they felt white supremacist pride.

In the twentieth century, this complex emotional link between feelings of class shame and race pride has made it extraordinarily difficult for civil rights leaders to think of white supremacists from the lower classes as race as well as class victims of white America. In addition, race-baiting politicians and pundits have found it easy to use these workers' race feelings of white pride to exploit them economically. I will illustrate these points by analyzing the strategies of Martin Luther King Jr.; former Alabama governor George C. Wallace; and Robert H. Bork, the conservative legal scholar and jurist, whose nomination to the Supreme Court by President Reagan was defeated by the collective efforts of liberal legislators, social activists, and civil rights groups.

## "The Shame of America"

Martin Luther King Jr. made a modern attempt to tally the wages *for* whiteness in economic, moral, and religious terms. These reckonings led King, less than a week before his assassination, to confess to an aide that "[t]ruly America is much, much sicker...than I realized when I first began working in 1955."[11]

King began by tallying the cost to white labor for a subjugated Negro worker. The fact that 75 percent of employed Negroes held menial jobs, King noted in his 1967 book *Where Do We Go from Here: Chaos or Community?* was a *requirement* of an economic system that needed a steady supply of "low-paid, underskilled, immobile labor for hand assembly factories, hospitals, service industries, housework [and] agricultural operations." This cheap Negro labor, King observed, held down the wages of the white worker and as a result made the wage scales in the South significantly lower than in the North.[12] Racial prejudice thus put poor whites in the ironic position of fighting not only against the Negro but also against themselves. White supremacy, King wryly noted, can feed the egos of poor whites but not their stomachs.[13]

King used this class analysis as the basis for a national agenda. His plans for a 1968 national "Poor People's Campaign" called the white poor to form a class alliance across color lines against an entrenched American ruling class.[14] His goal was not reform but a nonviolent revolution — a point conveniently ignored by the late twentieth-century, popularized national image of King. Wrote King:

> The dispossessed of this nation — the poor, both white and Negro — live in a cruelly unjust society. They must organize a revolution against that injustice, not against the lives of the persons who are their fellow citizens, but against the structures through which the society is refusing to take means which have been called for, and which are at hand, to lift the load of poverty.[15]

King believed that he was part of a black revolution that

> is much more than a struggle for the rights of Negroes. It is
> forcing America to face all of its interrelated flaws — racism,
> poverty, militarism, and materialism. It is exposing evils that
> are rooted deeply in the whole structure of our society.[16]

By 1968, King had declared that "[w]e are engaged in a class
struggle"[17] and called upon poor whites to transcend their racial
identity and unite in a common class struggle with the Negro. American capitalism must be confronted, he argued, because its ordering
of human affairs

> has often left a gulf between superfluous wealth and abject pov-
> erty, has created conditions permitting necessities to be taken
> from the many to give luxuries to the few, and has encour-
> aged smallhearted men to become cold and conscienceless so
> that, like Dives before Lazarus, they are unmoved by suffering,
> poverty-stricken humanity.[18]

Most white Americans did not heed King's call but, rather, reaffirmed their bonds to the racial and economic status quo.[19] King
described the white retreat from a structural critique as the consequence of an "inner conflict which measures cautiously the impact
of any change on the status quo." Peering deep into the content of
this inner conflict, King was forced to conclude that "white America is not ... psychologically organized to close the gap" between the
existing economic realities of the Negro's life and the goal of equality.[20] King also had to acknowledge that most whites would not seek
economic justice to improve their own condition if the uplift of the
Negro was entailed in such a venture.

This psychological condition that King discovered in whites led
him to talk about Negro shame and white guilt. For King, the
"shame of America" was its mistreatment of the Negro — the twice
forgotten man in America whose groans were not heard and whose
needs were not felt until he found the means to state his case in
the public square.[21] The problem, King said, was white racism:
the total estrangement of the body not only from the mind but
also from the spirit. He called such splinterings of the self a "con-
genital deformity" of racism. His prescription was redemption: the
white American's humble acknowledgment of guilt and an honest
knowledge of the self.[22]

Such talk of whites' need to atone for their participation in the "shame of America" could not plumb the depths of white Americans' own sense of racial victimization. Yet without such an exploration, King could not adequately explain the white rage released during the modern protest era. King's oversight became glaring when he took his civil rights campaign to the North, declared a "war on slums," and began his 1965–66 campaign in Chicago for open housing. He was brought to a rude awakening. The hostility of the white mobs King and his nonviolent protesters faced as they began their walk through the white Gage Park and Chicago Lawn neighborhoods literally stunned him.

David Garrow gives a vivid account of this Chicago scene in his book *Bearing the Cross: Martin Luther King, Jr., and the Southern Christian Leadership Conference*:

> The hostile whites... were already in position and armed with stones when the lead cars of the procession pulled into the center of Marquette Park. Police cars surrounded King as he stepped from the first car, but seconds later he was knocked to one knee by a rock that struck him on his right temple. Aides rushed to his side as photographers snapped pictures, and King knelt with his head bent for several moments before being helped to his feet. The blow had dazed him, though not drawn blood, and he appeared "visibly shaken" as more stones rained down and aides shielded him. After a pause, King steadied himself and the procession got underway as bottles and bricks continued to fly despite police efforts to control the crowd. "I had expected some hostility, but not this enormity," King told reporters. The angry mob trailed the marchers as they walked, and at the end of the protest, the final tolls showed forty-one arrests and thirty injuries. King declared that he had "never seen anything so hostile and so hateful as I've seen here today," but said he would march again, stones or no stones. "I have to do this — to expose myself — to bring this hate into the open."[23]

Not only was King forced to realize that the legislative and judicial changes brought about through Negro protest between 1954 and 1965 had been superficial rather than substantial and had done little to improve the lives of Negroes in the northern ghettoes, but he was also forced to realize that an era of counterrevolution had begun.[24]

The civil rights movement, urban riots, and Black Power militancy of the 1960s repeatedly exposed the white American as a deeply shamed being. The swift response of rage was a self-protective strategy of someone who was being taunted and humiliated — *again*. King could not find the source of this white rage because he had assessed this white shame from the standpoint of Negro shame and dignity.

King's failure to understand the depths of white shame entailed three basic factors. First and foremost was his own experiences of the transformative power of "unmerited suffering." Although he was repeatedly imprisoned, his home bombed twice, and he and his family constantly barraged by death threats during the southern stage of the protest campaign for Negro rights, King strove to find redemption in his humiliation and feelings of shame. He recognized the "necessity for suffering" and strove to "make of it [the] virtue" of love. For King, such suffering "served to shape [his own] thinking" by providing him with opportunities for transfiguring experiences.[25]

Second, King believed that the Negro protesters could transform the humiliation of their own unmerited suffering into dignity. Speaking of the 1955–56 Montgomery bus boycott, King said:

I do not wish to give the impression that nonviolence will accomplish miracles overnight. Men are not easily moved from their mental ruts or purged of their prejudiced and irrational feelings. When the underprivileged demand freedom, the privileged at first react with bitterness and resistance. Even when the demands are couched in nonviolent terms, the initial response is substantially the same. I am sure that many of our white brothers in Montgomery and throughout the South are still bitter toward the Negro leaders, even though these leaders have sought to follow a way of love and nonviolence. But the nonviolent approach does something to the hearts and souls of those committed to it. It gives them new self-respect. It calls up resources of strength and courage that they did not know they had. Finally, it so stirs the conscience of the opponent that reconciliation becomes a reality.[26]

The protesters' active struggle for dignity naturally led King to talk about white privilege — the wages *of* whiteness, which had cost the Negro dearly. King had good reason to believe that the experience of public humiliation could strengthen and mend the heart of the nonviolent protester whose dignity had been broken by unjust laws and social practices. He had the hard evidence of his own experiences and empirical observations.

Third, King drew an additional, and questionable, conclusion based on this data: that the newfound courage, esteem, and dignity of the Negro protester would stir the moral conscience of whites. He assumed that intensified relations with Negro, nonviolent protesters would force white Americans to discover the moral cost to themselves — the wages *for* whiteness — of their mistreatment of the Negro. According to King, whites, by supporting or acquiescing to racism, "had rejected the very center of their own ethical professions."[27] This center must be re-stimulated by the Negro protester so that it could be healed. In other words, King assessed the psychological cost of becoming white as a morally damaged core brought on by the white's mistreatment of the Negro.[28] Overlooked in this analysis was a more original damage to the core sense of self — the experience of feeling diminished by one's own white community.

King strove to stir "the conscience of the opponent"[29] not to defeat or humiliate an enemy but to win friendship and understanding.[30] These stirrings, however, poked at a self that had already been racially abused. The response was the self-protective strategy of rage.

King knew the social history of this rage: the early decisions to create a white supremacist culture first in the American colonies and then in the new nation. He, in fact, traced the roots of the racial delusions of grandeur of lower-class, white Americans back to slavery. King wrote:

> Generally we think of white supremacist views as having their origins with the unlettered, underprivileged, poorer class whites. But the social obstetricians who presided at the birth of racist views in our country were from the aristocracy: rich merchants, influential clergymen, men of medial science, historians and political scientists from some of the leading universities in the nation. With such a distinguished company of the elite working so assiduously to disseminate racist views, what was there to inspire poor, illiterate, unskilled white farmers to think otherwise?[31]

This cultural system of racist dogma, King argued, was established to convince white Americans that an economically profitable slave system was morally justifiable.[32] It is here, however, that King

overlooked the legacy of a psychological effect on poorer whites
of this cultural strategy to justify, explain, affirm, and perpetuate
slavery: shame.

As we demonstrated in chapter 3, the legal system created to support slavery was designed, in part, to split the lower classes along
newly created racial lines. In fact, these laws made all members of the
newly created "white race" tacit or active supporters of slavery and
thus established a viable means for the social control of "whites."

The effects of this inside job on "whites" fractured the self of
poorer whites, not because they were racists and thus filled with
guilt but, quite the contrary, because they were not racists — or at
least not so *by nature*. To learn to be a racist, this "whited" self had
to split off its own class interests from its racial identity. This self-
fracturing process created a racial self that was its own class enemy.
The white worker, now split against its own interests, felt diminished. This experience of diminishment is one way of characterizing
the personal experience of shame.[33]

These feelings of diminishment (a wage *for* whiteness) were con-
trolled by training "whites" to attend to and benefit from the tasks
of maintaining a slave-based society (a wage *of* whiteness). It is from
this perspective of the cost exacted from "whites" for the right to
be white that we can make sense of American historian Winthrop
Jordan's point that the colonial slave codes told "the white man,
not the Negro, what he must do": punish runaways, prevent as-
semblages of slaves, enforce curfews, sit on special courts, and ride
patrols. The result was a constructed consent among the masses
to support the slave system and a manufactured public dialogue
between masters and white men in general to confirm a sense of
mastery not only over black slaves but also over their own feelings
for the purposes of control. Such lessons were, in effect, an induction process into whiteness — a system that had the makings of a
"lockstep discipline."[34]

This socialization process, in effect, created whites. Legal scholar
Ian F. Haney Lopez makes this subtle and important point in
his book *White by Law: The Legal Construction of Race,* when
he claims that "[l]aw constructs race."[35] This legal construction
of race, Haney Lopez argues, is achieved by making abstract beliefs concrete through a system of discriminatory laws that create
and maintain material differences based on a premise of racial
domination and subordination. Once these laws have created and

perpetuated a "lived reality of material inequality," this reality then becomes a proof text for the belief that the "races" are indeed unequal.[36] This self-fulfilling, legal, discriminatory process creates what it legislates: "whites."

This social construction of a "white" requires us to make a distinction between a person's core sense of self before and after its identity is defined as white. Before the white identity is established, this core sense of self is not white. Its personal racial identity is, in effect, nonexistent because the socialization process has not yet been undertaken by its white community of caretakers, legislators, and police force. In other words, a new member of the white community who is self-defined as white has not yet been created.

The history of America's naturalization laws is an example of the way in which a white is created by law.[37] For much of the country's history, citizenship was restricted to "whites." Racial restrictions barring nonwhite, immigrant adults from achieving U.S. citizenship, in fact, were not completely dismantled until 1965.[38] In chapter 4, we examined one emotional fallout of this harrowing "whitening" process on European immigrants as well as native-born Euro-Americans: blackface minstrelsy.

American historian Leon F. Litwack in his book *North of Slavery: The Negro in the Free States 1790–1860* summarizes part of the general history of the restriction of citizenship to "whites."[39] Litwack writes:

> In 1790, Congress limited naturalization to white aliens; in 1792, it organized the militia and restricted enrollment to able-bodied white male citizens; in 1810, it excluded Negroes from carrying the United States mails; in 1820, it authorized the citizens of Washington, D.C., to elect "white" city officials and to adopt a code governing free Negroes and slaves.[40] Moreover, it repeatedly approved the admission of states whose constitutions severely restricted the legal rights of free Negroes.[41] On the basis of such legislation, it would appear that Congress had resolved to treat Negroes neither as citizens nor as aliens.[42]

This racial requirement for U.S. citizenship made evident a basic social fact about whiteness: it was an "entitlement." Legal scholar Cheryl Harris makes this complex point in her essay "Whiteness as Property," noting that

[t]he law's construction of whiteness defined and affirmed critical aspects of identity (who is white); of privilege (white benefits
accrue to that status); and, of property (what *legal* entitlements
arise from that status). Whiteness at various times signifies
and is deployed as identity, status, and property, sometimes
singularly, sometimes in tandem.[43]

Whiteness, like land, became a "property interest entitled to protection."[44] In short, it became a "vested interest."[45] This legal
"object" — whiteness — was both a requirement for and a personal
expectation of the "subject": the person who was entitled to think
of himself or herself as white.[46]

Costs as well as benefits were entailed in making, acquiring, and
protecting this personal investment in a white racial identity, and the
person who achieved this legal status became white by law rather
than by birth. This ability to both gain and lose one's whiteness
is evident in the fact that for most of America's history, a "white"
American woman who married a "nonwhite" alien was automati-
cally stripped of her U.S. citizenship.[47] It is not unreasonable to say
that she, in effect, through her marriage, lost her whiteness and thus
her right to be an American citizen.

This entire racialization process makes persons with white identities initially aware of the fact that the racial advantages they have
been given can be lost. For many "whites," however, this awareness that their whiteness can be lost cannot be retained in active
consciousness but, rather, becomes part of a racial system of white
denial: a vanishing point.

Legal scholar Barbara J. Flagg calls this "tendency for whiteness
to vanish from whites' self-perception the transparency phenomenon"[48] and argues that this "transparency" is "the defining characteristic of whiteness."[49] Whiteness, Flagg insists, "is always a salient
personal characteristic [for whites], but once identified, it fades almost instantaneously from white consciousness into transparency."[50]
Flagg describes this process but cannot adequately explain it.[51]

I am arguing that the process of becoming white is so quickly
relegated to, in Flagg's words, "the realm of the subconscious,"[52] because the process that creates this racial identity entails attacks upon
one's core sense of self by those who ostensibly love it the most: its
caretakers, legal defenders, and protectors. Such an awareness is too
much for most persons to retain in conscious memory.

I conclude that King and the modern civil rights movement exposed a self that had already been racially brutalized by its own white community. Its (racial) personhood had already been imposed through subordination.[53] The price *for* the right to be white had already been exacted: wholeness. What remained was a self that was conflicted and fearful of another racial assault. This fragmented, conflicted self would not normally think of itself as white, except when confronted by a "black" or some other racial "alien" — not because its whiteness was "transparent" and thus "unseen," as Flagg argues, but rather because the experience of becoming white was too traumatic to retain in consciousness.[54] Or the self exposed by the civil rights protesters was a "white" fixated on its whiteness (a self-proclaimed racist and white supremacist) as a defense strategy against more racial assaults from its own white community. In either case, King exposed the wounds of someone who had gone through a harrowing racialization process that produced a racial victim called a white person.

King did not understand the complex nature of this socialization process that turns a person into someone with a white racial identity — the content of which is the feeling of being at risk. He knew that his nonviolent campaign, as a method of bringing down America's legalized system of racial apartheid, had been a stunning success. As King said in his last book, *Where Do We Go from Here: Chaos or Community?* the strategy was "bold and crowned with successes." He admitted, however, that his own nonviolent strategies were "improvised and spontaneous," and he knew that the time had now come for sober reflection, a reassessment of methods, and a probe for deeper understanding. Otherwise, a people mired in oppression would never realize its own deliverance through the accumulation of power to enforce change.[55] King, in effect, by the end of his life, had become "uneasy and unhappy with his own philosophy."[56]

Not surprisingly, during King's own era and for the remainder of the twentieth century, America's public square became dominated by self-defined white men who were neither publicly uneasy nor unhappy with their own political philosophies and social theories about race. These "race men" explained to white Americans in graphic and incendiary terms why they should feel racially aggrieved: they had been shamed. *They* were the oppressed race; *they* were racial victims; *they* were being economically exploited; *they* were the ones who needed redress from their elected officials. This language made sense to the listeners because they did indeed feel racially abused and economically diminished. Rather than assess the social history of the racial and class assaults upon "whites" by their own racial kin, these white leaders used the feelings generated by this ongoing system of racial abuse within white America to exploit low-end white wage earners — yet again.

## The Assault

George Wallace knew exactly what he was doing as he took his race politics north in his 1964 presidential campaign. He knew, in short, how to work the fears of a *white* crowd and talk with them about the wages *for* whiteness. (He also knew how to celebrate with them the wages *of* whiteness, which seemed to be in imminent peril.)

Wallace, for example, used the language of the wages *for* whiteness to a predominantly male audience of seven hundred blue-collar workers who were deeply patriotic, *ethnic* Americans fiercely loyal to their own Polish, Czechoslovakian, Hungarian, and Yugoslavian neighborhood enclaves on the south side of Milwaukee. "This was Wallace country," social historian Dan T. Carter notes when describing this event in his book *The Politics of Rage: George Wallace, the Origins of the New Conservatism, and the Transformation of American Politics*. Wallace spoke to their fears and their rage. He talked about the threat to job security and the breakup of their communities that passage of Lyndon Johnson's Civil Rights Bill would bring: it "would destroy the union seniority system and impose racial quotas," make it "impossible for a home owner to sell his home to whomever he chose," and plunge the community's schools into chaos.[57] On this occasion, the Polish-American band sang "Dixie" in Polish.

His show, in effect, was twentieth-century minstrelsy without the grease paint. No grease paint was needed because the only character on stage was a white man. But this white man could evoke a twentieth-century version of Zip Coon and his plantation dandies with the skill of a consummate singer. Summarizing journalist Hunter Thompson's eyewitness report of the scene at one of Wallace's 1972 campaign rallies staged in Milwaukee's Serb Hall, Carter writes:

The air was electric. By the time Wallace was halfway through his speech the audience of Polish and Serbian Americans were stepping on his best lines, laughing, shouting, exhilarated by the furious energy of his snarling attacks against hippies, civil rights "agitators," welfare recipients, atheists, beatniks, antiwar protesters, Communists, street toughs who had "turned to rape and murder 'cause they didn't get enough broccoli when they were little boys." To a jaded Thompson, it was awe-inspiring, a political "Janis Joplin concert" in which "the bastard had somehow levitated himself and was hovering over us."[58]

Not surprisingly, Carter writes, the white reporters who covered such gatherings were often unnerved by this "nakedly primitive power of Wallace's rallies." The votes followed the audience's enthusiasm. In the April 1964 Democratic primary in Wisconsin, Wallace won 266,000 votes, more than a third of the 780,000 ballots cast in the state. His votes, as Carter notes, came from every section of the white population, taking a quarter of the votes from every major identifiable white group in the state. The "typical" Wallace voter was just as likely to be a member of a suburban Rotary club as a resident in an "ethnic" urban precinct.[59]

If, on the one hand, these election results are considered from the standpoint of the wages *of* whiteness, the numbers are puzzling. How to explain the fact that a third of all voting white Democrats in Wisconsin, a state with "a small minority population and little visible urban racial conflict," had voted for what the *New York Times* called "an anachronistic Southern demagogue"?[60] If, on the other hand, we set aside talk of white privilege and focus attention on the wages *for* whiteness, we find the story of a racial victim. The emotional content of this narrative will be the smoldering rage and endemic fear of the prospect of another racial assault.

Wallace sang the country blues of abuse: if the Civil Rights Bill became law, the Negro "expects and apparently intends to *bludgeon* the majority of this country's citizens into giving him preferential treatment." Whites would not be able to walk the streets "without *fear of mugging, raping, killing or other physical assault.*" At stake was the "*safety* of our wives and children."[61]

In short, Wallace, the five-term governor of Alabama (counting the election of his wife, Lurleen, as a stand-in), who repeatedly convinced the whites of his own state that *they* and not blacks were the victim of oppression, carried this same message across the land while representing himself as the nation's white savior.[62] The heavy irony of his claim, observed Judge Roy Mayhall, one of Wallace's staunchest Alabama critics, was that "Goddam, we're at the bottom of everything you can find to be at the bottom of, and yet we gonna save the country. We lead the country in illiteracy, and syphilis, and yet we gonna lead the damn country out of the wilderness."[63] Wallace, however, rose to national prominence because he knew race was going to become the central issue of American politics,[64] and used it to promote his own political ambitions.[65]

American historian Dan Carter chronicles the speed with which northern Republican politicians learned Wallace's language. Richard Nixon, for example, during his 1968 presidential campaign began to talk about "law and order" in American cities. Carter describes Nixon's enthusiasm as he found such talk to be the right formula to speak to white fears of racial assault:

> That "hits it right on the nose," [Nixon] said enthusiastically [to his staff]. "It's all about law and order and the damn Negro–Puerto Rican groups out there." Nixon did not have to make the racial connection any more than would Ronald Reagan when he began one of his famous discourses on welfare queens using food stamps to buy porterhouse steaks. His audience was already primed to make that connection.[66]

Explicit racial language was supplanted in the following decades by the language of *symbolic prejudice:* "the socially acceptable rejection of minorities for ostensibly non-prejudicial reasons."[67] This is the contemporary vocabulary for white racial contempt.

Donald R. Kinder and Lynn M. Sanders developed the notion of *racial resentment* to describe the psychological presentment this language addresses. It is a mind-set they repeatedly encountered during their national survey of racial attitudes, the findings of which were published in their 1996 book, *Divided by Color: Racial Politics and Democratic Ideals*. They drew two basic conclusions from their fieldwork: white racial resentment toward black Americans is based not on objective fact but on a subjective fear. Additionally, this resentment is the "most potent force in white public opinion on race today."[68] Summarizing their findings, they list the symptoms of this psychosocial state of affairs:

[R]acial resentment is a coherent and stable system of beliefs and feelings; whites express less of it in the presence
of black Americans; racially resentful whites are much more
likely to consider themselves and their families threatened by
racial policies at work and school than are whites who express sympathetic views toward blacks — even though we can
find virtually no evidence that they are in fact more threatened; white Americans who express racial resentment also
subscribe to derogatory racial stereotypes (i.e., whites who say
that blacks could be as well off as whites if they only tried
are also inclined to believe that blacks are dangerous, lazy,
and stupid); and, finally, racial resentment reveals a great deal
about where white Americans stand on matters of race. When
it comes to school desegregation or federal assistance or affirmative action, nothing explains variation in white opinion as
well as racial resentment.[69]

This pervasive system of white racial resentment, Kinder and
Sanders conclude, has "racially encoded" white political thinking. Whites vote for their perceived race interest rather than for
the immediate economic and social well-being of themselves and
their own families.[70] Clearly, their objectively groundless fears make
these voters prime targets for manipulation by political and economic interests all too willing to use race-baiting tactics to achieve
their own ends.

Kinder and Sanders identify but cannot adequately explain the
problem. Other contemporary political scientists also describe the
problem. Social theorists Thomas Byrne Edsall and Mary D. Edsall,
for example, in their book *Chain Reaction: The Impact of Race,
Rights, and Taxes on American Politics*, identify the race obses-
sion in white American politics that makes white working-class and
middle-class Americans vote as if their economic interests are iden-
tical to those of the rich. This voting pattern, the Edsalls suggest, is
"all the more remarkable" because these voters' political allegiance
to Republican party economic strategies benefits not them but rather
the voters in the top half of the income distribution.[71]

Ex-conservative doyen Michael Lind also notes this racial obses-
sion in white American voting patterns. In *Up from Conservatism:
Why the Right Is Wrong for America*, Lind presents a detailed account of the way in which the antiblack sentiment of many white

American workers has been used with calculated intent to give the new Republican Party "a southern drawl."[72] Lind cannot, however, adequately explain the lure of the bait.

The end-of-the-century consummate master of race-baiting explanations for white racial resentment is conservative jurist and pundit Robert H. Bork. In his 1996 book, *Slouching towards Gomorrah: Modern Liberalism and the American Decline,* Bork argues that the only truly oppressed group in America today is his own group: white, heterosexual males. He rejects the "rhetoric of victimhood" — whites seeking absolution from blacks — and looks upon this legacy of the modern protest era as another indication of the modern denigration of the white race.[73]

Bork's vocabulary is developed according to his most basic understanding of human nature: it is savage. "Every new generation," he writes, "constitutes a wave of savages who must be civilized by their families, schools, and churches."[74] The social and institutional constraints traditionally imposed on the American child thus both shape and repress.[75] Without such a process, civilization would be impossible.

This analysis not only displays Bork's own attitude toward the child's acculturation but also allows him to affirm the acculturated aspects of the child as civil and to decry the unacculturated parts as savage. From this perspective, it is easy to understand Bork's decision as a Yale law professor in the 1960s to ignore a "summons" from the Black Law Students Union (BLSU) to the Yale law faculty to appear in the faculty lounge.[76] These students, Bork suggests, in a furtive attempt to hold on to their self-respect in an academic environment that exceeded their abilities, chose "to reject both the standards by which they were judged and the faculty that judge[d] them." A friend and colleague, Alexander Bickel, attended the meeting and gave Bork an account that he summarized thus:

> The faculty sat in folding chairs that had been set out for them; the BLSU stood before them like instructors — very angry instructors — before a class.... In violently obscene language, the BLSU leaders berated the faculty which sat submissively in their chairs and took it.... When the BLSU was gone, a prominent member of the faculty turned to Alexander Bickel, from whom I had this account, and said, "Wasn't that wonderful! They were so sincere!" Bickel did not speak to the man for almost a year.[77]

Bork objected to such student tactics not because they were used by militant *black* students ("[w]hite radicals behaved no better," he said), but because the tactics exposed unfettered human nature — in this case a lustful, envious desire to acquire the rightful belongings of others. The pretense was egalitarianism, Bork claims, but in truth the real motivation was "envy" on the part of persons unwilling to admit the limits of their inherent, individual, genetic endowments.[78]

Applying theories about raw human nature and the function of America's social institutions, Bork concludes that the era of the 1960s "was against the entire American culture."[79] Bork, in fact, dates the "birth of the sixties" to a public declaration written by the Students for a Democratic Society at their convention held at the AFL-CIO camp at Port Huron, Michigan.[80] Bork focuses on the declaration in this document that humans are "infinitely precious and possessed of unfulfilled capacities for reason, freedom, and love."

Bork hotly disputes the students' belief that "human nature is infinitely malleable so that a new, better, and perhaps perfect nature can be produced by the rearrangement of social institutions." That is the dangerously misguided notion of all totalitarian movements, he writes, because humans resist attempts to remake their natures. Therefore, to fulfill the Port Huron vision, "coercion and ultimately, violence will be required."[81] Furthermore, such tactics would inadvertently expose the savage lurking in every human breast, and if sustained, would unleash the beast. Student attempts to expose the innards of others during the 1960s were thus deemed by Bork to be not only adolescent but, much more ominously, destructive and ultimately nihilistic.[82]

In short, these students had "rejected America."[83] The Port Huron document was "four-square against the nature of human beings and features of the world that are unchangeable." Human nature is not malleable; it is fixed. Unguarded exposures of human nature thus reveal and release the beast: the uncivilized human impulses and shameless sins of unchecked aggressive drives and lustful desires.[84]

Bork continues. In the 1990s, modern liberalism is simply the "mature stage" of the adolescent, nihilistic perspective of the 1960s. Its ideology is empty at the core.[85] It celebrates freedom, the pursuit of individual happiness, and the breaking of traditional social constraints on humans to keep their untoward impulses in check. This mistaken view of human nature, handed down to the contemporary era from the Enlightenment founders of liberalism, "has brought us to this — an increasing number of alienated, restless individuals, individuals without strong ties to others, except in the pursuit of ever more degraded distractions and sensations. And liberalism has no corrective within itself; all it can do is endorse more liberty and demand more rights."[86]

By contrast with maladjusted liberals, Bork can extol the virtues of successfully socialized American, heterosexual, white men, who have willingly submitted to the "traditional cultural values of the West"; have played by the rules, following the dictates of family, religion, and school; and, in fact, he infers, have represented these values because traditionally this group has been identified with them.[87]

Some of these men immediately enter the workforce after high school, but others want to go to college and make it by following the traditional paths open to them by merit, attending the best schools to get the best jobs their talents will allow them to secure.[88] But their reward for this dutiful submission to the mores and values of their society is gall: their interests have been undermined by the desires of lustful, envious, unacculturated individuals who are given educational and employment opportunities they neither merit nor deserve.

A case in point: blacks who do not meet the merit standards for entrée into the highest realms of America's education, government, and business worlds but who demand and are given such positions through affirmative action quota systems. Such systems discriminate against white men because they give special privilege to persons who no longer need them. In short, the modern civil rights movement succeeded in freeing blacks from legal racial discrimination: legalized discrimination no longer exists except as "mere wisps" of its former self.[89] Laws requiring such discrimination have been rescinded, and a system of government agencies has been established to protect and seek redress for anyone who charges illegal discrimination.

The claim that discrimination is structural — that is, built into social and economic structures — rather than apparent, Bork reasons, simply concedes his point. "Structural theories," he writes, "are simply an admission that actual discrimination cannot be shown, coupled with an unsupported assertion that it must nevertheless be pervasive. Only modern liberals and people with a vested interest in discovering racism would advance such an empty theory."[90] According to Bork, charges of structural racism against America's traditional institutions "are merely silly." If there were such endemic problems in America, Bork concludes, they would have manifested themselves as a series of individual acts of discrimination.[91]

Such claims of structural discrimination, Bork insists, are an "empty theory," mere speculation. In his book *The Tempting of America: The Political Seduction of the Law,* Bork argues that people who make such claims are, by definition, alienated from America's social institutions, and "[p]eople who are alienated obviously will not respect the basic institutions of a society they regard as illegitimate. Lectures about the right of self-government, judicial restraint, and the separation of powers will seem irrelevant if not reactionary."[92] Such persons would displace "democratic choice by moral principle"[93] with the activist agendas of private, individual interests. Individual interests do not a morality make for Bork. Quite the contrary. They lead to anarchy. The real victims of structural discrimination, for Bork, suffer because they have gone along with the institutions that have structured their lives as sanctioned by America's traditional values. One group so suffers: white, heterosexual males.

To illustrate this point, Bork offers vignettes of hapless whites, male and female, being publicly humiliated and silenced by blacks and their white, liberal, elitist supporters: white academics disciplined for challenging the erroneous historical claims of Afrocentrists; obsequious whites who seek absolution for the sins of the Jim Crow and slavery eras; and a particularly graphic story of the public humiliation of a white, female professor during a "faculty sensitivity session" at the University of Cincinnati. During this faculty session, a "woman was forced to stand up and be mocked as 'a member of the privileged white elite' because she was blonde, blue-eyed, and well educated. The trainer implied that her three degrees from prestigious private schools were not really earned but were a genetic entitlement. When the trainer later ordered her to stand up again, presumably to be abused once more, she could only sit and sob. Not one of her one hundred colleagues who were present came to her defense."[94]

Bork links such humiliating white experiences to the "deep, almost ineradicable, sickness of [American] culture," a sickness turned against white, heterosexual males. Reflecting upon the overall state of the race, Bork concludes that "[w]e have become a submissive people." This is "particularly true of whites where race is an issue."[95] What is particular noteworthy here is Bork's generalization about white humiliation. According to Bork, this incident with the woman is indicative of a white people who have submitted passively to their own racial degradation brought on by blacks.

Bork's major point is that white, heterosexual men are caught in a double bind. They had to submit to America's social institutions. Otherwise, they would have remained savages. But by having conformed and become their society's (parents', schools', religious institutions') ideal, civilized, successfully socialized human beings, they are then dismissed and replaced by persons who have not submitted to this same acculturation process. The heterosexual, white man thus suffers and is oppressed because of who he is: an exemplar of America's core values.

For Bork to reason otherwise, he would have to argue that America's social institutions are part of many white men's problem. Such an account might begin with six harsh facts about America's "booming" economy:

1. In the United States, 20 percent of the people own more than 80 percent of the wealth.

2. During the 1980s, the average family's income dropped almost 10 percent.

3. More than forty-three million jobs have been erased in the United States since 1979. Between 1993 and 1995, one out of every fourteen Americans lost her or his job.[96]

4. Although the jobless rate in the United States plunged to 4.3 percent in April 1998, the lowest it had been in three decades, wages also fell as the economy rebounded in the 1990s. "The median weekly wage, adjusted for inflation, fell in each of the first five years of the recovery, rising modestly for the first time in 1997."[97]

5. Numerous companies are opting to lower standards for job qualifications for their workforce rather than raise wages and thus cut into profits.[98]

6. Jobs paying $50,000 a year or more have twice the share of the job-loss that they had in the 1980s.

Next, such an account might go on to note that the result of these trends is the most acute job insecurity since the Great Depression. As economist Paul Krugman has pointedly argued in the November 3,

1997, edition of the *New Republic,* the modern success story of America's booming economy rests on the bent back of the American worker. The economy is booming because wages, the main component of business costs, are not going up. And wages are not going up because the American worker is presently too fearful to stand up and make demands. Downsizing has shaken worker confidence. Unemployment insurance lasts only a few months, and the global labor market has undermined the workers' bargaining power. These three basic economic facts, Krugman argues, have created one basic psychological fact for the typical American worker: anxiety.[99]

Finally, the account would have to note that the workers defined by this anxiety are largely high-end blue-collar and low- to middle-end white-collar workers who have acquired the trappings of middle-class success without the financial security needed to assure their continued membership in that class.

Such accounts have been given. Former Republican strategist Kevin Phillips, for example, notes in his book *The Politics of Rich and Poor: Wealth and the American Electorate in the Reagan Aftermath,* "For *all* workers, white-collar as well as blue-collar, their real average weekly wage — calculated in constant 1977 dollars — fell from $191.41 in 1972 to $171.07 in 1986."[100] The workers continue to lose ground today or are running as fast as they can in order to stay in place. But the "treadmill strategy" for financial security does not work for this anxious class of Americans because the gap between the wealthy and the rest continues to widen. Phillips, observing the aftermath of the "second Gilded Age" in America, as he calls the 1980s, trenchantly notes that "if two or three million Americans were in clover — and another thirty to thirty-five million were justifiably pleased with their circumstances in the late 1980s — a large number were facing deteriorating personal or family incomes or a vague but troubling sense of harder times ahead."[101] Or as one economist forthrightly notes when describing the labor climate in the 1990s, "A lot of employers have grown accustomed to a culture in which they don't need to give real wage increases to hire and hold workers."[102]

Simply stated, Americans are well aware of the fact that the Gilded Age of the 1980s made the rich richer, the poor poorer, and the middle class anxious. A strong economy no longer means job security for most middle-class Americans — and they know it. This awareness, however, has not produced a rebellion among the lower classes against the rich but, rather, has generated a frenzied attempt to keep up the appearance of being part of the elite class. But such appearances include a penalty: debt. In short, as the gap between the wealthy and the lower 80 percent of the population widened in the 1980s and the salaries of the middle class fell, the spending habits of the middle class rose.

Social theorist Juliet B. Schor identifies this overlooked consumer pattern in middle-class spending in her book *The Overspent American: Upscaling, Downshifting, and the New Consumer,* and reminds us that

> the competitive upscale consumption that began in the 1980s, with the attendant expansion of the American dream, wasn't invented by Nancy Reagan and it wasn't a cultural accident. It was created by the escalating lifestyles of the most affluent and the need that many others felt to meet that standard, irrespective of their financial ability to maintain such a lifestyle.... The story of the eighties and nineties is that millions of Americans ended the period having more but feeling poor. Nearly all the pundits missed this dynamic, recognizing only the income trends or the spending increases.[103]

This pattern of overspending by America's middle-class "poor" has been easy to overlook for a basic reason: white shame. Neither the dominant race factor entailed in this buying pattern for most of these Americans nor the emotional condition these Americans exhibited was taken into account. This conceptual failure occurred because the experience of race shame, as we have seen repeatedly throughout this book, is not traditionally associated with *white* Americans.

Contemporary shame theorist Andrew P. Morrison's own work unintentionally illustrates this problem. He associates race shame in America with the shame engendered in African Americans because they are "often judged by white American society as inferior." To reinforce this point, Morrison notes further that "[l]ong-standing, deeply simmering shame has accompanied the African American experience since slavery."[104]

Morrison, however, also notes the "ethnic" feelings of shame engendered, for example, in Jewish Americans because they are often held in contempt by the dominant American religious group: Christians. The experience Morrison wants to elucidate using such examples is *difference* and the feelings of self-hatred it can generate in a person. Morrison thus notes the "connection between self-hatred about ethnic origin, cultural heritage, and feelings of being different," and gives his readers a rule: *"When an individual speaks of feeling different from a given cultural or social norm, we should wonder whether the language of shame is behind this expression."*[105] This shame rule entails two elements: personal feelings of difference and an analysis of these feelings for possible expressions of shame experiences.

We can use these two elements to identify both the race and shame factors in Juliet Schor's general discussion of the "overspent" American.

### The Feeling of Being Different from a Given Cultural or Social Norm

The social norm for most overspent Americans is persons whom they respect, share similar values with, and wish to emulate. Juliet Schor, reflecting upon the nature of this standard reference group, notes that "many of us are continually comparing our own lifestyle and possessions to those of a select group of people we respect and want to be like, people whose sense of what's important in life seems close to our own."[106] This reference group for most Americans, Schor notes, is the upper middle class, whose members earn between $72,000 and $91,000 per year: 15 percent of the American population. This is the group, Schor tells us, "that defines material success, luxury, and comfort for nearly every category below it. It is the visible lifestyle to which most aspiring Americans aspire."[107] Schor, in effect, has described the *white* lifestyle norm for white Americans. That other racialized groups also might aspire to this lifestyle is not disputed. I am making a separate point: most of the persons Schor describes in her book as "status buying" are white. A case in point. In one of the rare passages in her book in which she directly confronts this "white race" factor head on, Schor notes that "Caucasian women were much more likely to engage in status purchasing than African Americans or non-Caucasian Hispanics. . . . [C]ontrolling for income, African Americans saved more."[108]

Like Morrison, Schor can most easily conceptualize this problematic spending pattern in racial terms when describing status buying by inner-city children or America's poorest persons who seek "to compensate for their racial and economic exclusion."[109] She does not conceptualize status spending, however, as a white middle-class problem for Euro-Americans who are trying to compensate for their own experiences of racial exploitation and economic exclusion from the privileges and lifestyle of the white elite. Schor moves close to this insight without conceptualizing it when she speaks of the fear by these (white) Americans of "dropping down." Writes Schor:

> The dirty little secret of American society is that not everyone did become middle-class. We have the rich and poor and grada- tions in between. Class background and income level affect not only the obvious — if and where you go to college, the quality of your children's elementary school, the kind of job you get — but also your likelihood of getting heart disease, the way you talk, and how respectfully you're treated by others.... At all levels, a structure of inequality injects insecurity and fear into our psyches. The penalties of dropping down are perhaps the most powerful psychological hooks that keep us keeping up, even as the heights get dizzying.[110]

Clearly, the "dirty little secret" that Schor refers to in this citation most immediately refers to white self-consciousness since whites and not blacks or other racialized minorities in this country are supposed to be middle-class as a racial entitlement. The entitlement to middle-class economic status, as Cheryl Harris notes in her essay "Whiteness as Property," is the "core characteristic of whiteness." This class sta- tus is "the legal legitimation of expectations of power and control that enshrine the status quo as a neutral baseline, while masking the maintenance of white privilege and domination."[111]

Simply stated, it is no secret that most black Americans are not middle-class. Yet it seems to be a "dirty little secret" that this is also the case for most white Americans. They, too, are not comfortably ensconced in this class. Middle-class poor whites who overspend to create the illusion of economic success and stability are thus, in a certain sense, financially recapitulating the legal history of their own racial creation. In effect, they are disempowering themselves as a class for the sake of a constructed appearance. As Schor notes, "[A] central feature of American consumer life [is that] what people spend both reflects social inequalities and helps to reproduce and even cre- ate those distinctions."[112] Consumption, in short, is both a source and indicator of social distinction.[113] The result of this social cre- ation for the white middle-class poor, however, is white wage slavery in which these wage earners owe their souls to the company store. To quote Schor:

- Between a quarter and 30 percent of households live paycheck to paycheck;

- In 1995, one-third of families whose heads were college-educated did no saving;

- In 1995, the median value of household financial assets was a mere $9,950.[114]

These wage earners also actively participate in their own economic demise in another way: they impoverish their own local communities. Schor calls this impoverishment of their own social and cultural environment a "boomerang effect on the public purse and collective consumption." This effect works by forcing wage earners to pay for services privately that they have refused to pay for publicly. Schor chronicles this process, noting that

[a]s the pressures on private spending have escalated, support for public goods, and for paying taxes, has eroded. Education, social services, public safety, recreation, and culture are being squeezed. The deterioration of public goods then adds even more pressure to spend privately. People respond to inadequate public services by enrolling their children in private schools, buying security systems, and spending time at Discovery Zones rather than the local playground.[115]

This process is a collective act of class suicide because these overspent Americans are actively participating in the demise of their own class's needs, interests, and requirements for a healthy, viable social environment.

What drives this mad dash to the bottom by the white, middle-class poor? What is behind this fear of "dropping down" that, in effect, turns poorer "whites" into foes of their own class interests? Using Morrison's shame rule, we must wonder whether this fear of appearing different from the white elite entails feelings of shame. Such a consideration is particularly compelling because, as we have seen throughout American history, one "psychological hook" that links poorer "whites" to the interests and lifestyles of the rich is shame. More precisely, white shame.

*The Language of Shame*

Schor notes that the zealousness of overspent consumers entails an active construction of their personal identities. To underscore this point, Schor uses the lecture comments of the chairman of a multi-national consumer-products corporation who notes that "[w]e are what we wear, what we eat, what we drive. Each of us in this room is a walking compendium of brands. The collection of brands we choose to assemble around us have become amongst the most direct expressions of our individuality — or more precisely, our deep psychological need to identify ourselves with others."[116] Schor notes that this psychological need to identify with one's reference status group turns the apparent drive for social differentiation through competitive spending into its opposite: a "continuing social ritual" in which one repeatedly tries to be like everyone else. As one advertiser quoted by Schor notes: "Although people may claim that they are striving for individuality, they all end up looking more or less predictably the same."[117]

This entire process, Schor concludes, entails a certain psychological compulsion that can absorb consciousness and become a substitute for other activities. In short, it can become obsessive and "[start] to take over your life."[118]

Do these buying patterns conceal a race-based language of shame for overspent Euro-Americans? To even begin to answer this question, we need a contemporary psychological primer, one that enables us to understand the mental and emotional terms that link race and class identity in white America to the elite. We must understand what is so threatening about difference. We must talk about the core sense of self, and we must understand what we mean when we talk about anxiety. Only then can we determine whether middle-class poverty is a price of admission for many Euro-American members of the lower classes to the white race in America.

# SIX

# A PRIMER

Each of us has a personal "sense of a core self" that cannot be thought, touched, directly addressed, or seen.[1] We need a primer, a set of psychological concepts, to understand how this sense of self is impaired by an American social process that forces Euro-Americans to become "white" in order to survive.

## The Sense of a Core Self

You will note the presence of your own sense of a core self if you consider what happens as you read these words and hold this page, becoming aware through touch of the page's smooth surface and through sight of the dark figures on the background, and through thought of the ideas to which these sensations give rise. The act of coordinating these disparate mental and sensate events into one coherent moment of personal experience is your sense of a core self. Its presence is your awareness of what you naturally do as a human being: you relate.[2]

The pioneering work of developmental psychologist Daniel N. Stern contains a description of an infant's sense of a core self in contemporary psychoanalytic terms. As Stern notes in his book *The Interpersonal World of the Infant: A View from Psychoanalysis and Developmental Psychology*, by the age of two or three months, the infant has a sense of itself as a separate, physical, coherent being with its own feelings and physical history. "This self generally operates outside of awareness. It is an experiential sense of self," Stern says, "that I call the *sense of a core self* [and] is a perspective that rests upon the working of many interpersonal capacities."[3]

This sense of a core self, Stern suggests, is also a sense of being related to another being with a core sense of self. In short, it is a sense of being both distinct from and also related to but not fused with someone with a different core sense of self.[4]

Stern, who also refers to this sense of self as our "physical self"[5] and the "existential bedrock of interpersonal relations,"[6] describes this sense of being related to and yet discrete from others as the integration of four basic experiences — our sense of coherency, agency, patterns of inner feeling (affect), and personal history. In order to emphasize this relational quality, developmental psychologist George Butterworth calls this experiential sense of self-coherence and integrity the "ecological self."[7] In short, we are always part of the natural world and an expression of our social world — even when we are alone.

This relational nature of our core or "nuclear self" led Heinz Kohut, the founder of self-psychology, to declare that "autonomy is impossible" because to be a self is to be in relationship with others as part of one's own self-defining feelings. Said another way, one's sense of a core self occurs in a matrix of relationships in which an "I" experiences a "You."[8] Once this sense of a core self is achieved, human experience operates in *a domain of core-relatedness.*[9]

Strictly speaking, we should not even call this sense of a core self an "it,"[10] because we are referring to a moment of relating, an act of life. Butterworth emphasizes the noncognizability of this activity, noting that this "core self is neither a cognitive construct, nor a concept of self, nor linguistic or even self knowledge. It is the foundation, in perception, action, and emotion, for the more elaborated aspects of self that are yet to be developed."[11]

In adults, this core activity of relating is a given. As Stern notes, we take it for granted. In infants, however, we immediately notice the presence of this core ability to relate when we smile and the infant smiles back.[12] If we respond with an even broader smile, so, too, will the infant, and these moments of affect-based responses and actions will crescendo into laughter.

Through numerous similar experiences, the infant learns that other core selves can regulate its own moods, but it never forgets that its experiences are its own, so that its sense of being a discrete entity does not collapse as a result of such interactions. Why? The basic answer is *difference.*[13] The infant's core sense of self is not ruptured because of the difference between its expectation of what its caretaker will do and what the caretaker actually does.

The erasure of this difference is often a psychological requirement for "making it" in white America.

## Difference

An easy way to think about the infant's experience of difference is to recall our own experience when we pick up a package that we assumed was heavier that it actually is. As we pick up the package, we are mildly startled by the difference between the actual weight and our expectation of what it would weigh, and so we make a series of muscular and mental adjustments in order to handle the actual weight.

Every day, we repeatedly make such muscular and mental adjustments to engage a world that exceeds our conceptual grasp until we engage it with our senses. We then adjust our grasp symbolically and sentiently in an interplay of encounters between ourselves and the world in which we are both astir and stirred.[14]

Our grasp of the world, quite literally, takes place in this realm of difference between ourselves and that which is beyond our subjective experiences, thoughts, expectations, and estimations. In this domain, we negotiate our world; we navigate human experience. It is here that engagement occurs. Here human relationship is both formed and experienced. This realm *is* the locus of engagement between self and another. It is an intermediate area of experiencing,[15] our "we-go"[16] (as opposed to the isolated "ego" that classic Freudians conceived as part of the discrete, private personality structure of an isolated and autonomous self). This realm of difference is the self that is always more than itself alone because its sense of itself includes an awareness of the world of nature and other human beings who are different from but participate in and alter its own core acts of relating.

Stern's concept of a sense of a core self highlights the difference between the infant's sense of a core self and that of its caretaker. This difference occurs because the infant's caretaker is not the same as the infant's core self.[17] The difference shows itself as the unpredictability to the infant of the caretaker's behavior. Human encounters are virtually impossible without this difference, as Stern illustrates in the following example:

Suppose that an infant experienced joyful cycles of antici-
pation and resolution only with mother, and that mother
always regulated these cycles in the *exact* same way (virtually impossible). That infant would be in a tricky spot. In this
particular, unchanging activity, mother would be sensed as a
core other because her behavior would obey most of the laws
(agency, coherence, continuity) that specify others as against
selves. However, the infant could not be sure to what extent
his or her feeling state was an invariant property of self or
of mother's behavior since both would invariably accompany
this feeling.[18]

In this impossible situation, the mother's action would be indis-
tinguishable from the infant's expectation. Thus the infant would
have no unexpected feelings that alerted the infant to the presence of
another person who could not be reduced to its own expectations.
Stated technically, we could say that, in this case, the other could not
be taken into account "as a thing in itself"[19]— someone with an independent center of self-generating activity. Someone, in short, with
her or his own discrete way of relating to others. Instead, the infant
might feel as if it were relating only to itself.

We must now imagine an opposite scenario: the *adult* in the world
of the infant who cannot tolerate distinctions between itself and its
own child's feelings. Psychoanalytic theorist Alice Miller describes
this scenario in her book *Prisoners of Childhood: The Drama of the
Gifted Child and the Search for the True Self*. For the child to develop a healthy sense of autonomy and self-esteem, the parent must
be completely aware of the child as its own center of activity and
must also take this center seriously and admire it.[20] The parent,
in short, must not retaliate when the child acts differently from its
parent's expectations.

Parents should train and instruct the child, Miller insists, but not
based on the giving and withholding of affection. Such a strategy is
cruel because it injures a "child's tender, budding self." Miller writes:

It is very fortunate when our children are aware of this [cruel]
situation and are able to tell us about it, for this may enable
them to throw off the chains of power, discrimination, and
scorn that have been handed on for generations. When our
children can consciously experience their early helplessness and
narcissistic rage they will no longer need to ward off their help-

lessness, in turn, with exercise of power over others. In most cases, however, one's own childhood suffering remains affectively inaccessible and thus forms the hidden source of new and sometimes very subtle humiliation in the next generation.[21]

Miller's basic point is that the child needs to be loved unconditionally. But this seems practically impossible to a great many adults, who have not experienced this kind of unconditional affirmation during their own childhood and thus cannot provide such an affirmation for their own child. Furthermore, such parents then seek an object for the gratification of their own unmet need for affirmation as a core center of relational activity. Simply stated, they desperately seek another self to affirm them and to recognize them. Not surprisingly, they turn to their own children for this affirmation.[22]

Newborn babies, as Miller notes, are ideal for fulfilling this parental need because they are "completely dependent on [parents], and since [parental] caring is essential to [their] existence," they do all they can to avoid losing their parents.[23]

Thus, from the very first day onward, infants will muster all their resources to this end, like a small plant that turns toward the sun in order to survive.[24] Adapting its needs and its sense of itself entirely to its caretaker, however, keeps the child from developing its own independent sense of a core self. This is problematic because the child, as we have seen, is actually more than these parental expectations. It has its own core center of relational activity that is different from its parent's expectations.

Accordingly, the child suppresses its sense of feeling different and denies its own personal sense of history that does not conform to its parent's expectations, thus impairing the child's core ability to relate while keeping its own integrity. The emotions, affections, sensations, tones, moods, attitudes, and so much more that fill every moment with an irreplaceable presence called "me" — as an unrepeatable instant called "now" — are lost. Unable to live out its own acts of feeling, the child does not develop a true self (its own feelings) that differ from its parent's expectations. Rather, the child will conform its needs and actions to the parent's needs. Differences between parental expectation and the child's expressions are compromised and begin to disappear.

The child thus becomes a figment of the parent's imagination, a false self. It becomes, in short, the perfect child, someone who conforms uncomplainingly to what others think. The cost of this conformity is that everything that is uniquely different about the child's sense of its own core self is threatened. Differences are deadened, hidden, denied, or in some way neglected. This self-annihilation of difference can be called the "self's Armageddon," the "self's civil war."[25] When the remains — that is, the lack of self-coherency and integration — of this self-demolition process are discovered by the conscious self, this self, seeing its own broken-ness, feels shame.

## Shame

A precise psychological description of this internal civil war called shame is given by Heinz Kohut:

> The exhibitionistic surface of the body-self, the skin,...shows ...not the pleasant warmth of successful exhibitionism, but heat and blushing side by side with pallor. It is this disorganized mixture of massive discharge (tension decrease) and blockage (tension increase) in the area of exhibitionistic libido that is experienced as shame.[26]

In other words, the parts of the self that have not been consistently lovingly and empathically affirmed because they are different from what the caretaker expected are "split off" from the child's oper-ative, conscious activities of engagement with others or separated from it through repression. We call these split-off feelings of one's self an abridgment of one's ability to relate wholly and coherently to the world in which we must live.

The experience of shame, however, has its source in more than the sense of a core self overwhelmed by the child's original outreach that was not empathically affirmed by its parents and thus became the split-off aspects of the self.[27] Shame also gives an account of the failure of the self to live up to its own ideals. These feelings of failure are internally induced; no external "shamer" is necessary. The self has not been humiliated, exposed, neglected, or abused by another. Rather, the feelings of shame-filled dejection, apathy, and depression have been brought on by the self's failed attempt to live up to its own notion of an *ideal self*.

This ideal self, psychoanalytic shame theorist Andrew P. Morrison argues, is the child's idealized parental image. It reflects the child's own developmental movement toward engagement and affiliation with its caretakers,[28] now expressed intrapsychically as an ideal self-image.

Two extended studies taken from real life will make this rather technical description of shame as well as the concepts of difference and the sense of a core self easier to grasp. We begin with personal experiences recounted by Bill McCartney, the former Colorado University football coach who in 1991 founded the Promise Keepers, the evangelical Christian men's movement that has been described as the fastest growing religious revival movement in the United States in the past one hundred years.[29]

## Study 1: Bill McCartney

McCartney's redaction of his own early attempt to doubt his father's wisdom gives us a vivid example of an abridgment of the difference between parent and child. McCartney recounts the story of the first time he attempted to hold his own with his father, an Irish, Catholic, Democrat, ex-Marine who was secretary-treasurer of his union local for twenty consecutive years. McCartney, at age fourteen, believed that he knew more than his father. Writes McCartney:

> Our first major difficulty came when I was about fourteen, when I was certain — for the first and only time in my life — that I knew more than my dad did. Just about the time I got pretty heavily into my cocky mode, he got very heavily into his silent mode.
>
> He finally froze me out. We didn't speak for six weeks.
>
> Finally, it not only dawned on me that I didn't have all the answers — but I felt so doggoned terrible! I just couldn't stand the silence any longer. When I showed the proper remorse and respect, things quickly got back to normal. As I look back on it, silence was my dad's best strategy.[30]

McCartney's father used the withdrawal of his love and affection for his son as a means to prevent the child from experiencing separation from him. This is the dynamic of a toxic family system that obstructs individuation.[31] It impedes the child's attempt to express its own feelings — its differences with its own caretaking environment. Such a strategy can eventually destroy the realm of difference between the child and its parent and thus compromise the child's ability to make a distinction between how it feels and what others do. The child's blocked feelings must now be vigilantly patrolled and monitored for any movement toward escape. Monitoring can entail drugs. Escape can take on the force of rage.

It is interesting to note here that on the same page McCartney recounts this altercation with his father, he also describes both his anger and frustration — that is, his temper, which he acknowledges is notorious and frequently uncontrollable. He also introduces the reader to the beginning of his problem with alcoholism during his senior year in high school.

Without attempting to present a case study of McCartney's overall personality, we can clearly see that his father's withdrawal of affection to "freeze out" his son's own attempt at difference was won with punishing success. The son became like his father. McCartney, by his own admission, also has a dominant personality. Authority, not introspection, is his personal mode.[32] He is called "coach" by his Promise Keepers for good reason. The line of authority he affirms is hierarchical and absolute. Such posturing leads us to look for hidden feelings of shame.

McCartney, without using the word *shame*, lists the classic characteristics of this conflicted state of the self in his 1997 autobiography, *Sold Out: Becoming Man Enough to Make a Difference*.[33] McCartney writes: "I still battle insecurity, the sullen belief that deep down I'm unlovable. I trace it back to drinking, to internalized taunts I weathered as the undersized freshman linebacker at Missouri. They are deep waters too deep and choppy for me to navigate solo."[34]

Concerning his motives for success, McCartney admits that "[u]nderlying it all, I was still motivated by insecurity, by that need to win, to succeed."[35] Intimacy, for him, was experienced as a threat, and so he did everything he could to avoid intimacy with his wife and children. McCartney says he knew that "his actions didn't match [his] convictions," and thus he felt both empty and miserable.[36]

All of these experiences suggest the presence of shame.[37] They also lead us to predict that the content of his white racial identity will entail feelings of shame when he discovers, in a racial context, his broken ability to relate. A racial incident that happened to

McCartney in the mid-1980s demonstrates this point. By his own account, he discovered a hitherto unknown depth of pain, sorrow, and suffering within himself.

McCartney went to the funeral of Teddy Woods, a highly respected African American attorney in Denver who had been a star football player at Colorado University and who had died at age forty. Although Woods had graduated before McCartney became the team's coach, McCartney felt it part of sports protocol to attend the funeral.

Arriving early at the funeral, McCartney sat at the front of the church, which was soon packed with a predominantly African American congregation. McCartney knew no one present. I shall let McCartney's own words describe what happened next:

> What happened to me that day changed my life. It may be hard for you to understand, but when I sat down and started listening to the music, *I was deeply affected.* The mournful singing of the mostly black congregation expressed a level of pain I hadn't seen or *felt* before. As I looked from side to side across the crowd, I realized that their grief over the loss of Teddy Woods was *bringing to the surface* an even deeper hurt. This wasn't just a funeral; it was also a gathering of *wounded, long-suffering believers.*
>
> *In response, I began to weep uncontrollably. I tried to cover my tears, fearing someone would see that I barely knew Teddy Woods.* I thought they might accuse me of grandstanding to gain acceptance and approval in the inner city — a recruiting ploy. *Yet I couldn't hold the tears. The grieving and groaning exceeded anything I had ever experienced. I have never been the same since then.*[38] [emphasis added]

McCartney's account has three structural elements entailed in an experience of shame:

- *The self-discovery of a hidden, discordant feeling.* McCartney discovered a feeling, a level of pain within himself, that he had not previously felt. This discovery challenged McCartney's conscious sense of the nature and content of his emotional life.

- *The removal of the barrier to difference between self and other and the experience of the domain of core relatedness.* McCartney's feelings of pain as a wounded, long-suffering person mingled with the pain of other long-suffering persons in the church. His own suffering was both touched off and validated through the stirring music and liturgy of the church service in the midst of a group he had learned to believe he could never belong to: black America.

- *Flooding and psychic paralysis.* McCartney struggled to hold back the tears but could not do so. He engaged in a self–civil war. His lost battle to stave off feelings of distress was an acknowledgment of the vastness of his own grief over an un-named loss. His attempt to get his feelings back under control was an acknowledgment of the full range of feelings he could not afford to have.

It is fitting that during a funeral McCartney discovered his own buried feelings, parts of himself that had not survived his own so-cialization process. The tension, dissonance, and discord induced by this discovery were unbearable for McCartney. He could not stay with his feelings. To get an objective handle on them, McCartney, a born-again Christian from an Irish-Catholic background, turned to Christian theology for assistance, taking three basic steps.

*First, McCartney gave his personal pain an external, black, human source.* Reflecting upon the pain he experienced during the funeral, he concluded that he had felt the black racial pain of the congregants who were mourning the injuries they had suffered as a result of white racism. According to McCartney, he had "come in touch, for the first time, with the pain, struggle, despair, and anguish of the black people. Stunned by that experience, I felt a great desire to understand what I had observed. I also wanted to pursue what I had felt in my spirit."[39] We shall return to his subjective endeavor.

*Second, McCartney explored this external source by interviewing his black friends.* "I began," he said, "to question black people I had known for years." By means of this process he listened to an array of personal recollections that revealed "dramatic experiences and everyday examples of the injustices [faced as] black Americans."[40]

*Third, he turned to an assessment of his own internal state and concluded that the internal meaning of his pain is guilt for acts of white racist complicity.* McCartney, in other words, believes that the depth of pain he felt while in relationship to the black congregants must have resulted from his awareness as a white man of the acts he had done to cause them pain. (He does not, however, mention any

specific racist acts that he had committed.) He concludes that he and
other white Christians are racists. Writes McCartney:

> We've stood against a lot of other social evils, but we have not
> stood against racism and called it what it is: sin!...We should
> feel conviction deep in our souls for this sin. The damage is
> incalculable. The toll is immeasurable. We should drop to our
> knees before Almighty God in repentance.[41]

McCartney, by transforming his feelings of shame into a recogni-
tion of white guilt for the sin of white racism, has turned both white
racism and his own white racial identity into an affair that can be
handled only by God and his Son because sin, McCartney believes,
is conquered by God through Christ.

McCartney, by means of this strategy, can explain the difference
between his conscious mental image of himself and the content of
his own feelings as a sin that no human effort can rectify. This
is the case because difference, for McCartney, is the domain of
Satan. Why Satan?

In Promise Keepers biblical lore and morality, which claims that
the Bible is "without error in the original manuscripts" as God's
written revelation to man, Satan is the devil (Rev. 12:9), the serpent
that tempts men to turn against God's command (Gen. 3:1–24), the
tormentor of Jesus (2 Cor. 12:7),[42] the one who desires to destroy
the work of Christ in the world.[43] Satan is a demonic force dead
set on one goal: to dethrone God by instilling personal doubt in be-
lievers about the efficacy of God's own character and commands.
The work of the Christian is thus to resist any impulse to personal
doubt in God's efficacy and commands. Following this logic, racism,
according to McCartney, is "Satan's stronghold" because it causes
Christians to doubt the efficacy of God's commanding presence and
it impairs the ability of Christians from different racial backgrounds
to work together to spread God's word.

Two nonracial examples of McCartney's use of this idea of Satan
will make McCartney's own emotional antipathy toward difference clear.

• *McCartney's reaction to his protracted marriage problems.* According to his wife, Lyndi, the first thirty years of their marriage was
a downhill slide. She and Bill did not stop and take inventory of
their lives together. She felt woefully neglected by the exigencies of
her husband's coaching career and admits that for years she was de-

pressed, thought of divorce, and, in her words, went through some bad times during which she could only see the bad stuff. McCartney, in contrast, thought that the contention and discord, and his wife's doubts about the efficacy of their marriage, had their source in Satan. Lyndi McCartney writes:

> Bill thought we were being attacked by Satan, but I was certain it was coming from the Lord. I think He was sick of watching us do things our way. He loved us enough to try to and shake us up.
> We went to a counselor.[44]

McCartney's use of Satan to explain his marital discord is an effort to find an external demonic source for the internal discord he experienced in his married life. An alternative approach would have let him assess his own emotional life and engage his wife as someone with a different and equally important center of activity.[45]

• *McCartney's reaction to his detractors.* According to McCartney, his detractors were acting at the behest of Satan. He writes:

> Satan has worked tirelessly to thwart our efforts — none of us are naive about that. Since taking on the vision of Promise Keepers, I've been insulted, cursed, and even spat at during my daily walks through campus. I've received a mountain of hate mail through the years. Editors have attacked me every step of the way, and cartoonists have had a great time with their caricatures. But I'm committed to keeping the faith and keeping the dream alive, regardless of the persecution. I never believed that following Jesus was going to be easy.[46]

In short, anyone who challenges *McCartney's* views and resists his interpretations of experience by proffering a different set of viewpoints and experiences is described by McCartney as a messenger of Satan.

Further, when Satan is present, so McCartney argues, humans' efforts to reconcile themselves to God are of no avail. This is the case because only Christ can fend off the demonic tempter of humans so that they can be reconciled with God. By turning racism into a "sin" and thus consigning it to the domain of Satan, McCartney can now conclude that social engineering to counter racism is futile.

This conclusion is the heart and soul of the Christian right's protest against liberal government policies and programs intended to improve the downtrodden. Writes McCartney:

> Society tries in vain. Government efforts are losing ground. Defeat swallows mankind's best ideas. May every church plead in unison for God's heart and God's solution to bring reconciliation. May our prayer warriors work overtime. Let the pulse of the Body of Christ quicken and not rest until we see change. And let it begin with you and me.[47]

One of the black leaders in Promise Keepers, Tony Evans, picks up the same theme when he writes:

> Let's face it! Economics is no excuse for promiscuity and irresponsibility. And racism doesn't get teenage girls pregnant.
> The fact is, if Dad doesn't provide spiritual responsible leadership in the home, baby is in big trouble. That's what the folks downtown don't understand. Without strong families built on a framework of biblical morality, there is no sum of money — no federal, state, county, or municipal program — that can get us out of the ditch we've fallen into.
> How do we break the cycle? By getting men to assume their responsibilities and take back the reins of spiritually pure leadership God intended us to hold. Otherwise, our culture is lost.[48]

Such reasoning is endemic to the Christian right. This logic, which extracts racial issues and personal crises from their social contexts, is found, for example, in *Active Faith,* the book by the first executive director of the Christian Coalition, Ralph Reed. He writes:

> In the inner city illegitimacy is rampant, drug deals are openly conducted on street corners, hopelessness is the norm, and children are shot by marauding carloads of juvenile gang members. There is no economic solution to this social chaos — it is a collection of moral problems that require moral solutions.[49]

The profamily religious right, Reed tells us, has grown and prospered addressing these "purely moral" problems. From this nontemporal, socially disembodied perspective, which turns social problems into a spiritual fight against demonic forces for the sake of the human soul, Reed, like McCartney, not only can affirm his stand against racism but also can argue that he is following a religious path forged by Martin Luther King Jr. Reed, thus, can affirm his own stand against racism while sidestepping the economic issues for both black and white Americans that King knew were inextricably interwoven with the race issue in America.[50]

King, as we saw in chapter 5, would have found such sentiment antithetical to his claim that the "inseparable twin of racial injustice is economic injustice."[51] King, thus, would have rejected Reed's claimed allegiance to the principles of the civil rights movement.

McCartney puts the solution to white racism in America in God's hands and in those of the "prayer warriors" who endeavor to change the hearts of individual men through prayer and good deeds. He does so by stripping white racism of its roots in human abuse. As a result, whiteness is left unexplored as a seat of racial abuse against both Euro-Americans and African Americans. *This racial strategy deals with what one does racially as a white but not with what was done to oneself in order to make one think of oneself as a white. This absence of attention to the emotional abuse that makes it difficult for someone to relate wholeheartedly to another person obscures the hidden injuries to Euro-Americans within their own communities. It is those very injuries that, when discovered, produce feelings of shame and, in a racial context, white shame.*

What is particularly vicious and problematic about McCartney's approach, and that of other Christian right organizations such as the Christian Coalition, is that objectors to this strategy of covering up problems of abuse within Euro-American families and communities are called Antichrists, satanic forces intent upon dethroning God. Genuine conversation becomes, in a word, impossible.

McCartney can thus be unflinching in referring to his white followers as white racists who must repent, and he can insist upon his ongoing effort to work "aggressively at addressing the issue of racism head on."[52] The message is hard-hitting and relentless. It is also irrelevant to the personal lives of the men who are attracted to the rallies. They are there to deal head-on with shame issues in their private lives. For these men, racism is not an issue of shame in their private lives.

As one man named Samuel, a fast-food restaurant manager who attends Promise Keepers events, said in protest against this emphasis: "They're hitting it too hard. I'm just trying to repair my marriage and learn how to be a better father, and these guys want to dump all this guilt on me for racial sins of the past. I don't have the time or the energy for that."[53] Because white shame issues are kept exterior to a private realm of shame concerns, the white self-image of the participants in Promise Keepers remains essentially unchallenged. The psychological foundation of the racial status quo in America remains intact.

McCartney's strategy thus maintains a white racial identity, albeit a guilty one. This white guilt, however, is remaindered to the realm of Satan and sin. Once it is in this realm, it can be expunged by Christ — or at least its "sting" can be blunted. What remains is a man with a white racial self-identity desensitized to his own unresolved feelings from the painful awareness of his complicity in racist acts. Such a man emerges from this process with an arrogant Christian self-assurance. In the words of Promise Keepers staffer Tony Evans, such a man does not ask, he takes.[54]

From this particular religious perspective of Christian sin and shame, we can now make more sense of the claim by Robert H. Bork that the core sense of self is savage.

## A Christian Theology of Shame

As we saw in chapter 5, Bork insists that white heterosexual men are the only oppressed group in America today. Bork believes that this problem can be resolved only by a reinstatement of traditional social and religious constraints. According to Bork, "the rise of an energetic, optimistic, and politically sophisticated religious conservatism" is indeed the most promising hope in contemporary America, and Bork calls for the replenishment of the public square with religious faith, the faith of "a demanding God, a God who dictates how one should live and puts a great many bodily and psychological pleasures off limits."[55]

Bork argues that this is what the American people (as opposed to their "elitist" liberal leaders) desire. The facts speak for themselves, he says. The evangelical denominations that promote Bork's traditional values — "that make the highest demands on their members, that focus on salvation, community, and morality, that stand against the direction of the secular"[56] — are gaining members, while the more permissive mainline Protestant churches have melded with the far left wing of secular culture and thus lost members.[57] The absence of traditional values in the secular culture, Bork concludes, is "the empty space" out of which spring our rising crime rates, high divorce and illegitimacy rates, and the nihilism of modern, secular American life.

To fully understand what kind of religious and political-social control Bork is calling for, we must place his reasoning in its Calvinist tradition — more precisely, the Calvinist-based Puritan view of human nature upon which the American nation was founded.[58] Bork's moral reasoning both affirms and exemplifies this tradition. Take, for example, Bork's belief that the liberal's objections to economic inequality are prompted by envy; or his contention that the refusal to recognize that other people are wiser, richer, more intelligent, and more powerful than oneself is likewise the product of envy. People must accept that there is justice in a system in which others have outpaced them.[59] The founders of liberalism, Bork concludes, "would have done better had they remembered original sin."[60]

All this is an updated version of Calvin's belief that man's merit is God-given and not manmade. (In today's terms, Bork calls such native, individual ability one's "gene pool.") Calvin, for example, in his *Institutes of the Christian Religion,* enjoined men to esteem, regard, and honor men who have more than themselves because God has freely bestowed these special gifts of honor upon the elect. Thus, the "poor must yield to the rich; the common folk, to the nobles; the servants, to their masters; the unlearned, to the educated" unselfishly, without envy and with high regard for their social superiors. This reverence for others, Calvin tells us, is accomplished by "unremittingly examining our faults [and calling] ourselves back to humility." In the absence of such self-denying practices, "there are either the foulest vices [which] rage without shame or if there is any semblance of virtue, it is vitiated by depraved lusting after glory." Calvin believes that self-knowledge is the discovery by man of his human nature befouled by sin — a lustful, envious, and depraved human nature of a fallen man in a fallen world. Devotion to God is a practice of self-denial, the aspersion of the filth of one's own nature as enjoined by Christ for the glory of God.[61]

This is a theology of shame and can be traced from Calvin back to Augustine, the fifth-century Catholic bishop who gave the Catholic Church its first official doctrine on human nature, a doctrine of original sin that has at its core a theory that blames the victim for its own brokenness rather than the social order that assaulted it. Augustine used the Genesis story of Adam and Eve to construct and explain his shame theology.[62] His argument entails three basic steps.

First, Augustine argues that Adam and Eve were naked, knew it, and were not ashamed before they sinned. Augustine makes this assertion based on the biblical claim that their eyes were opened (Gen. 3:7 — they saw the fruit) and they knew that they were naked and were not ashamed (Gen. 2:25). They were not ashamed of their own bodies, Augustine argues, because a "garment of grace" covered the couple's genitals.[63]

Second, Augustine argues that *after* the couple sinned and countered God's command, God fit the punishment to the crime: *"[T]hey were stripped of [their garment of] grace, that their disobedience might be punished by fit retribution."* As a result of this loss of God's grace, Adam had an unwilled erection. In Augustine words, there began in the movement of their bodily members "a shameless novelty which made nakedness indecent."[64] Why did *these* bodily members move? Augustine's reasoning is true to form: the punishment God gave them fit the crime — insolent insubordination. Insolence begot insolence. Adam's inferior member acted on its own and for its own satisfaction, rose up, so to speak, against its superior (Adam's will).

Third, the couple thus covered their nakedness because they felt shame: the involuntary movements of their genitals made their nakedness indecent. Augustine concludes that sexual pleasure and any inordinate desire (lust) that causes humans to fall into sensuous, delirious pleasure and delight rather than cling to God are "accompanied with a shame-begetting penalty of sin."[65]

To understand why Augustine constructed a theological explanation of shame that links it to feelings of guilt for a sinful act, we must remember that he was a particular kind of realist — one without an edge of social criticism.[66] The shame theology Augustine bequeathed to the Christian West is a doctrine that had made peace with a Roman world of pervasive human suffering framed by a profound sense of personal alienation.[67]

Augustinian scholar Peter Brown trenchantly makes this point in his book *The Body and Society: Men, Women, and Sexual Renunciation in Early Christianity*, when he notes that Augustine's Paradise began to look like the hierarchical order affirmed by the Roman state, where the bonds that held subjects to emperors, slaves to masters, wives to husbands, and children to parents could neither be ignored nor abandoned.[68] Augustine did not turn a deaf ear to the "terrible cascade of helpless misery, of ignorance, arrogance, malice and violence [that] set up a deafening roar." But in Augustine's theology of shame,[69] the sound and fury of broken souls lost their objective source—the social order—and were pinned on an internal source: man's own willfulness, his disobedient pride.[70]

Augustine's realism without an edge of social criticism fully informs Calvin's Reformation theology, which construes shame as a virtue: the virtue of acknowledging that one is a sinner and lacks all grace save that bestowed by God upon a broken and befouled human nature. The Puritan view of human nature reaffirmed this Christian doctrine, calling human nature "a gulf of grief, a sty of filthiness," "bogs of Filth," "Lumps of Lewdness," "Slough and Slime," and "sullied flesh" requiring a "holy despair in ourselves."[71] Richard Baxter, an eighteenth-century Puritan, encapsulated this view of fallen human nature in his *Christian Directory:*

> Man's fall was his turning from God to himself; and his regeneration consisteth in the turning of him from himself to God.... [Hence,] self-denial and the love of God are all [one]. ...Understand this and you will understand what original and actual sin is, and what grace and duty are.... It is self that the Scripture principally speaks against.... The very names of Self and Own, should sound in the watchful Christian's ears as very terrible, wakening words, that are next to the names of sin and satan.[72]

This degraded, "fallen" human self, so this reasoning goes, must be rejected by man for the sake of his soul.

Shame toward one's own human nature thus became an indication of a sinner, but a repentant sinner. As American historian Sacvan Bercovitch notes in his book *The Puritan Origins of the American Self*, this Puritan struggle to separate the self from its own nature and strive toward God is the basis of the self's internal civil war. The Puritans both sanctioned and required such an "internal Armageddon," a self–civil war in which the love of Christ requires one to loathe the self.[73] This psychology, Bercovitch suggests, is in keeping with the call by the Calvinist doctrines out of which the Puritan mind emerged to "rid our selves of all selfe-trust." This call not only resounded throughout American Puritan literature, Bercovitch concludes, but became the leitmotif for the traditional moral values and religious persuasions of the "American self."[74]

This received tradition of Christian shame theology makes the victim solely responsible for his or her own brokenness. Such a strategy is akin to slapping a child because the child has been raped by its own parent. Bork's use of such theological reasoning limits his explanation of the socioeconomic degradation of white heterosexual men to two perspectives: either they are oppressed by the envy of others ("blacks," "feminists," and other persons who have not been adequately socialized), or they do not merit more because they were not among the elect chosen by God (via one's gene pool). Nowhere in Bork's scenario is there a place for the harm a "white" man (or woman) suffers because he (or she) submitted to a socialization process that compromises one's ability to relate with integrity to others. Nor is there mention of the harm caused by class wars waged by the rich against everyone else.

## Study 2: Martha C. Nussbaum

Our second study of the way the denial of difference between child and parent can influence the structure of one's racial identity is taken from the contemporary work of a woman who represents progressive (rather than conservative) thought in white America: University of Chicago philosopher Martha C. Nussbaum. In *Cultivating Humanity: A Classical Defense of Reform in Liberal Education*, Nussbaum describes an incident from her own early induction process into whiteness.[75] Her description of this incident deserves to be cited at length:

> In Bryn Mawr, Pennsylvania, in the early 1960s, I encountered black people only as domestic servants. There was a black girl my age named Hattie, daughter of the live-in help of an especially wealthy neighbor. One day, when I was about ten, we had been playing in the street and I asked her to come in for some lemonade. My father, who grew up in Georgia, exploded, telling me that I must never invite a black person into the house again. Nor was school very different: my private school included black people only as kitchen help, and we were encouraged to efface them from our minds when we studied. My history courses said little about slavery. Never, in high school or afterward at Wellesley and New York University, did I read

any work of literature by a black writer.... No music teacher among the many with whom I studied piano and voice mentioned jazz, and I hardly heard it until I was in my twenties, although it was a major source of more or less all the modern classical music (by Copeland, Ravel, Bernstein, Poulenc) that I did play and sing.

My career in philosophy has continued my segregated academic life. In my twenty years of teaching in departments of philosophy and classics I have taught only two black graduate students and have not had black colleagues. Now that I am in a law school, I have had two black colleagues — one of whom, a visiting professor, was one of my two black philosophy graduate students. Very few black students take nonrequired courses in philosophy, and even in my current law teaching I see few black faces. I find things out mostly by reading and imagining.[76]

Nussbaum has presented a vivid account of part of her formal racial induction process into whiteness: beginning with the emotional explosion of her father against *her* because she brought home a friend who was the wrong color. The emotional content of her racial identity, so our conceptual approach leads us to believe, probably contains her reaction to her father's anger against her and his threat to her well-being in *his home.*

To remain in his home, what feelings did the ten-year-old Nussbaum have to suppress? Nussbaum does not answer this question. Nor does she tell us how she felt or what she did with her feelings toward her friend after this incident. Did she continue to play with the girl? How did she feel about her own infraction of her father's race rules? Did her attitudes and feelings toward her father shift? Does she feel white shame when these ancient feelings are recalled and exposed?

Nussbaum never speaks of white shame, but she pointedly discusses "black shame" several times. When Nussbaum, for example, characterizes her students' discussions of Bigger Thomas, the protagonist in Richard Wright's novel *Native Son,* Bigger becomes the "symbol of white hatred and black shame."[77] The protagonist of Ralph Ellison's *Invisible Man* becomes "the poor, humiliated black boy."[78] Ellison's protagonist, as an adult, becomes someone whose "struggle with shame... will be unfamiliar to the white middle-class reader, who probably will not be able to identify with... an experience [of eating a yam in the street as a sign of race pride]. Such a failure of sympathy," Nussbaum tells us, "prompts a deeper and more pertinent kind of sympathy, as one sees that a human being who initially might have grown up free from the deforming experience of racism has been irrevocably shaped by that experience; and one does come to see that experience of being formed by oppression as a thing 'such as might happen' to oneself or someone one loves."[79]

Nussbaum's description of the initial failure of sympathy by the white, middle-class reader toward Ellison's protagonist is remarkable for several reasons. First, she overlooks her own experiences of racial oppression wrought by her father, who forced her to act white in order to stave off further parental explosions. Nussbaum was subsequently educationally "deformed" (that is, misinformed) by the racially restrictive system in which she was schooled.

Second, her lack of empathy with Ellison's character who eats a yam in public is particularly telling because Nussbaum, thirty-eight pages earlier, describes Diogenes the Cynic (404–323 B.C.E.) as habitually shocking "his Athenian contemporaries [by] eating in the public market place.... Only dogs, in this culture, tore away at their food in the full view of all."[80]

Nussbaum uses the latter example of public eating to demonstrate a strategy by Diogenes to help persons reflect upon their own deeply held feelings of prejudices "by making them consider how difficult it is to give good reasons for many of our deeply held feelings."[81] Nussbaum accepts the invitation to "consider ourselves citizens of the world" and become "philosophical exiles from our own ways of life, seeing them from the vantage point of the outsider and asking the questions an outsider is likely to ask about their meaning and function. Only this critical distance, Diogenes argued, makes one a philosopher."[82]

For Nussbaum, there are limits, however, to this freedom of philosophic reflection. Stoics, she tells us, "do not want us to behave as if differences between male and female, or between African and Roman, are morally insignificant. These differences can and do enjoin special obligations that all of us should execute, since we should all do our duties in the life we happen to have, rather than imagining that we are beings without location or memory."[83]

At the first level of this claim, Nussbaum's position is admirable because she is, after all, affirming difference as vital and positive in human relationships. But at a deeper level, it seems that this difference affirmed by Nussbaum is not fluid but fixed. This is the case because Nussbaum's account of rigid racial and sexual lines of distinction is counterfactual.

In the Greco-Roman world Nussbaum describes, a man, through the progressive loss of body heat, so the science of the day claimed, could become "womanish";[84] " 'soft' male bodies (*malthakoi* in Greek) acted like women... [and] belonged to the intermediate heat zones between very male and very female."[85] Behavioral codes were exacting because in this ancient world such sexual differences were not absolutely fixed. A boy, in effect, had to learn how to become and remain male. Although "[n]o man," as one scholar notes, "might actually become a woman,... each man trembled forever on the brink of becoming 'womanish.' "[86] Moreover, the differences between African and Roman were not absolute. Rome, after all, was an empire. Thus, Augustine, the North African bishop of Hippo, was a Roman citizen.

Nussbaum argues that racial categories are fixed: "[O]ne cannot in fact change one's race." One can simply imagine "what it is like to inhabit a race different from one's own."[87] Yet Nussbaum tells us that she is a "Jew," "a convert from Episcopalian Christianity," which meant that as a graduate student at Harvard in 1969, she could not have been married in Harvard's Memorial Church, "which had just refused to accept a Jewish wedding."[88]

Nussbaum's characterization of herself as a "Jew" is ironic in the context of her claim that one's racial identity is fixed. This is the case because the Jew's racial identity, in Europe, was not white but black. As Sander L. Gilman painstakingly demonstrates in *Jewish Self-Hatred,* Jews in Europe "became the blacks."[89] The male Jew and the male African were conceived of as equivalent threats to the white race.[90] Kafka noted in 1920 that as a Jew — from a European perspective — he had a Negro face.[91] Gilman notes in his book *Freud, Race, and Gender* that the "male Jew and the male African were seen as equivalent dangers to the 'white' races in the anti-Semitic literature of the late nineteenth century." Furthermore, the "general consensus in the ethnological literature of the late nineteenth century was that Jews had 'black' skin, or were at least 'swarthy.' "[92] By becoming a "Jew," Nussbaum, from this particular European racial perspective, changed her racial identity.

Nussbaum's claim of racial fixity also goes against the grain of contemporary race theory. As social psychologist James M. Jones notes in his taxonomy of race constructions, the genealogy of race has a geographic lineage. One of the major defining characteristics of race is its "geographical nature," rather than a putative blood type or physical appearance.[93] Numerous studies, as Jones notes in his account of race taxonomies, have indicated that the biological basis for racial categories is spurious and cannot be supported by objective scientific data. Race, in short, is not God-given, but man-made.

Physiologist Jared Diamond makes this point vividly in his re-categorization of physical traits as the basis for racial divisions. As Diamond notes, there are equally valid ways of defining races. Each procedure, however, would bring about a decidedly different outcome:

> One such procedure would group Italians and Greeks with most black Africans. It would classify Xhosas — the "black" group to which President Nelson Mandela belongs — with Swedes rather than Nigerians. Another equally valid procedure would place Swedes with Fulani (a Nigerian "black" group) and not with Italians, who would again be grouped with most other African blacks. Still another procedure would keep Swedes and Italians separate from all African blacks but would throw the Swedes and Italians into the same race as New Guineans and American Indians. Faced with such differing classifications, many anthropologists today conclude that one cannot recognize any human races at all.[94]

Racial classification systems, in short, are tautologies. Psychological studies of race, for example, first create the categories for the subject to be studied. These categories are then used to investigate the subjects predetermined by these categories. The investigations, however, are conducted as if the subjects are biologically rather than categorically predetermined to such places in the scientist's mind. The categories, Jones argues, are actually determined by "(a) how Whites have regarded members of other races as reflected in studies of prejudice, discrimination, and racism, and (b) how racial groups, primarily Blacks, have reacted to this perception and the disadvantages they have been subjected to over many years."[95] Nussbaum's claim of racial fixity is, in a word, anachronistic.

What is particularly interesting about Nussbaum's musings concerning black shame is the absence of her reflections on its racial counterpart in Euro-Americans: white shame. This absence is all the more remarkable because Nussbaum, as we noted above, described a series of personal incidents suggestive of ways in which she might have experienced white shame when she discovered the impairment to her own ability to relate wholeheartedly to others as she learned how to mentally "efface them."

We are left in the dark about Nussbaum's reflections on white shame. What is not left in doubt, however, is that Nussbaum was psychologically attacked by her father and mentally compromised by her teachers. These two conclusions provide us with the conceptual space needed to understand how rigid definitions of race and feelings of racial revulsion could evolve in Nussbaum without the necessity of having feelings of racism and bigotry accompany them.

An insight from psychoanalytic theorist D. W. Winnicott helps us find this place of analysis without judgment about the nature and structure of Nussbaum's white racial identity. *Anxiety,* Winnicott suggests, "is not a strong enough word" to describe the "primitive agonies" felt when one's own caretaker attacks one for being different. Rather than suffer these agonies, the child's sense of self-integrity disintegrates, and the child ceases to affirm its own discrete sense of efficacy and value.[96]

Nussbaum's resistance to the idea that racial definitions can be broken down, following Winnicott's logic, might pertain not to a future but to a past event that has been sentiently experienced but not fully acknowledged, in short, an embodied feeling that has been mentally effaced. This is the case because, when such racial experiences of breakthrough occurred in her life as a child and young adult, she could not mentally gather them into herself and psychically survive in either her father's household or the private schools she attended. This is the theory.

Is Nussbaum's rigid characterization of racial distinctions motivated by such an anxiety? In short, is it motivated by fear of another explosion by her father and thus another risk to the ten-year-old girl's sense of a core self? We do not know.

Nussbaum's account of her lessons in becoming white, however, demonstrate how a parent and an extended white community of teachers can partially kill a child's ability to relate with integrity when socialized as a "white." The outburst by Nussbaum's father against her constitutes an abuse of power because a child cannot survive either emotionally or physically without its caretaker's support. From the child's perspective, it thus does not have a choice. It

must conform or risk further abuse. It is difficult for a child to survive intact as a whole self in such a toxic emotional environment.
Nussbaum's story is thus the tale of a child at risk.[97] It is a story
of child abuse.

Applying Winnicott's thinking to Nussbaum's case, if this incident was the impetus for the further development of a white racial
identity, then such an identity had as a central emotional content
an "underlying agony" that remained "unthinkable"[98] and thus un-
named. I call the discovery of this agony in a racial context —
white shame.

•

In sum, our primer of psychological concepts allows us to examine the structure of a Euro-American's white racial identity as an
impaired sense of a core self, an inability to relate to others with
self-integrity. This impairment is the result of episodes in which a
person's difference from a white ideal was attacked by her or his own
caretaker(s). The white self-image that emerges from this process will
include the emotional fallout from the self-annihilating process that
created it: the breakup of one's own sense of coherency, efficacy,
and agency as a personal center of activity. Whenever the content
of this white racial image is exposed, white self-consciousness can
feel shame — and rage.

Concerning this rage, Heinz Kohut borrows a potent image from
modern physics to describe what happens when a core (or "nuclear")
self fragments because of a failure of its caretaking environment.
Writes Kohut: "Just as the splitting of the atomic nucleus...is followed by the appearance of an enormous quantity of energy, so does
the break-up of the self (the 'nuclear' self) lead to the appearance of
an isolated 'drive,' e.g., to the eruption of narcissistic rage."[99]

Obviously, one does not have to be a racist to display such rage
toward members of another racialized group. Such rage can flow
from the release of ancient feelings of fury against the persons who
originally assaulted the self for being different — one's own caretakers — now directed toward persons who have been racialized
as "different."

•

This theory has two immediate uses. First, we can explain the in-
visibility of white shame as a major race problem in white America.

This problem is not seen because the original source of the problem is overlooked: abuse against Euro-Americans for being different from their caretakers' expectations, desires, and needs. We began this book with stories of the vicissitudes of Euro-American children who had to learn how to become white. It is fitting that we have returned to such stories. In a country in which such children are taught to feel racially privileged, the racial cruelty they experience from their own white community becomes invisible. Alice Miller notes:

> The fountainhead of all contempt, all discrimination, is the more or less conscious, uncontrolled, and secret exercise of power over the child by the adult, which is tolerated by society (except in the case of murder or serious bodily harm). What adults do to their child's spirit is entirely their own affair. . . . But in twenty years' time these children will be adults who will have to pay it all back to their own children. They may then fight vigorously against cruelty "in the world" — and yet they will carry within themselves an experience of cruelty to which they have no access and which remains hidden behind their idealized picture of a happy childhood.[100]

Second, our primer can help us identify a self-compromising element in the drive by Euro-American, middle-class wage earners to eliminate the difference between themselves and their (class) superiors: the fear of appearing different from their upper-class assailants. To describe this class fear among Euro-Americans, we borrow two terms traditionally used to talk about interracial tensions between black and white Americans: race-passing and white flight.

## Race-Passing

"Passing," in traditional American parlance, refers to someone's attempt to shift the public perception of her or his racial identity. A brief example of passing will help us locate a self-destructive element in this racial ploy. Legal scholar Cheryl L. Harris gives us our example when describing her African American grandmother, who had "fair skin, straight hair, and aquiline features" and presented herself as a white woman in order to get a job as a sales clerk in a major Chicago retail store.[101]

This act of passing, Harris observes, had a certain "economic logic":

> [B]eing white automatically ensured higher economic returns in the short term, as well as greater economic, political and social security in the long run. Becoming white meant gaining access to a whole set of public and private privileges that materially and permanently guaranteed basic subsistence needs and, therefore, survival. Becoming white increased the possibility of controlling critical aspects of one's life rather than being the object of another's domination.[102]

There is a downside to this race-passing strategy, however, a price of admission to the "privilege" of being thought of as white: the loss of a sense of a core self. Harris's grandmother had to listen without protest to her white co-workers' and customers' remarks against black Americans. Harris refers to this silence as her grandmother's risk of "self-annihilation" whenever she engaged in the strategy that ensured her economic survival: passing.[103] In short, the wage *for* whiteness for Harris's grandmother was "complicit[y] in her own oppression" by abridging her ability to relate with a wholehearted integrity.

This personal price tag for her grandmother's success should not surprise us because we are already familiar with the cost:

- Norman Podhoretz, as we saw in chapter 2, referred to his price of admission into the realms of white power and privilege as the necessity of becoming a "facsimile WASP." This self-corrupting transaction led Podhoretz to an acquired distaste for his own ethnic background and many of the people whom he had loved.

- Frank Rissaro, as also noted in chapter 2, was ensconced in his white "middle-class world" that made him feel like an "illegitimate...pushy intruder" who did not deserve to be respected for what he had achieved.

The feelings of shame expressed by both Podhoretz and Rissaro reveal their complicity in the racial degradation of their own background as the price tag for economic advantage.

We highlight two basic elements entailed in Harris's story of her grandmother's race-passing strategy that are also found in the stories of Podhoretz and Rissaro as they "passed" beyond their ethnic and class backgrounds and entered the higher ranks of white, middle-class American life: the public desire for a better socioeconomic position and a private decision to risk annihilating their own core sense of personal history, coherency, and integrity.

The first element is easy to find and explain: class inequality. As economic theorist Juliet B. Schor observes in *The Overspent American: Upscaling, Downshifting, and the New Consumer,* the "classless-society and end-of-ideology literature of twenty-five years ago turns out to have been wishful thinking."[104] There are "deep class inequalities" in American society. This current economic state of affairs means that to make it today into one of the few slots open at the top, one must look, act, speak, and dress in a certain manner. Taste, Schor notes, "has economic ramifications. You can blow a job interview by exhibiting improper table manners at lunch, wearing the wrong outfit, or using language inappropriate to the station to which you are aspiring. Cultural capital can be used by those on the higher rungs of the ladder to devalue those below."[105]

Schor, in sum, argues that a person from the lower classes must pass beyond her or his original, lower-class economic conditions, mannerisms, and lifestyles in order to be a success. To achieve this end, one must take flight from one's own original background. Thus the second element in passing: flight. Jim Goad calls this move away from one's own roots and toward a white, upper-middle-class ideal an "oft-overlooked form of white flight."[106]

## White Flight

From what are Euro-Americans who engage in this activity fleeing? The most immediate economic answer is class exploitation.

Goad, in his 1997 book, *The Redneck Manifesto: America's Scapegoats: How We Got That Way and Why We're Not Going to Take It Anymore,* gives a thumbnail history of this exploitation. This bitter book about Goad's own "redneck" background and lifestyle is filled with enough racial, ethnic, and class invectives to offend virtually anyone who reads it. The book, however, is worth noting because Goad repeatedly reminds us of an oft-forgotten fact in American history: "The urge to enslave is truly color-blind."[107]

Goad's "Quick History of the White American Underclass" (chapter 3 of his book) is a crash course in upper-middle-class violence against the European servile and lower classes in early American history, as described in the work of contemporary historians.

We presented part of this history in chapter 2. Goad's work fills in more of the details needed to make sense of a fear that drives lower-class Euro-Americans to flee from their own class backgrounds:

- "[H]alf and possibly as many as two-thirds...of ALL white colonial immigrants arrived in chains."[108]

- "In Virginia and Maryland during the 1600s, the white-servant quotient was even higher. A study of Virginia from 1623 to 1637 showed that white servants outnumbered white freemen by three to one." The ratio was six to one in Maryland at one point during the 1600s.[109]

- "According to accounts from both Virginia and the West Indies during the 1600s, roughly EIGHTY PERCENT of white slaves/servants died within the first twelve months after arrival."[110]

- These indentured servants, which Goad calls "white temp-slaves," could not vote, sit on juries, or marry without their master's permission. Their "[s]o-called 'privileged' white skin was brutally ripped open on plantation after plantation."[111]

- "An indentured servant was legally 'the property of his Master,' as phrased by West Florida's Governor Johnstone in 1766. ...White servants were listed as property on tax returns alongside livestock, the chattel next to the cattle," which meant that they "were bought, sold, traded, and inherited like any other disposable goods."[112]

- "As with Africans, white families were frequently broken apart and sold to different bidders. At auctions, white servants were often purchased in bunches by men known as 'soul drivers,' who'd chained groups of newly arrived white slaves together and herded them on foot through rural areas, selling them at a profit."[113]

- "During a 1659 parliamentary debate on the white-servant trade to the colonies, legislators used the word 'slaves' rather than 'servants.'" Goad notes that "[a] Virginia law of 1705 mentions the 'care of all Christian slaves,' Christian being a contemporary euphemism for European." In 1751, a writer for *London Magazine* noted that "a British convict shipped overseas became a 'slave in America.'" Not surprisingly, "White indentured servants frequently referred to themselves as slaves."[114]

Goad's conclusion is both trenchant and short: "Economics. That's all it was, is, or ever will be. Racism is only a smoke screen, a cynical diversionary tactic. Once you understand that, the rest is easy."[115] His descriptions of the dire conditions of the indentured and then the freed "whites" and their progeny who remained trapped in the lower classes give vivid testimony to the exploitation of the laboring classes in America that we have repeatedly referred to throughout our own work as *classism*.

In sum, both poor whites and blacks were originally disciplined by the labor laws and practices of the upper classes. The consequences for defying these rules are vivified by American historical accounts that depict the punishment meted out to the black slave. Rarely noted is the psychological effect of this punishment on the psychic structure of the whites. Why?

American historian Winthrop D. Jordan provides a clue in his book *The White Man's Burden: Historical Origins of Racism in the United States*, when he describes the eighteenth-century treatment of slaves who violently resisted white authority:

The bodies of offenders were sometimes hanged in chains, or the severed head impaled upon a pole in some public places as a gruesome reminder to all passers-by that black hands must never be raised against white.[116]

The brutality and barbarity deployed against the slaves can obscure the effect of such acts on the white passerby. But as Jordan points out:

These instructive tableaux were not invented by the colonists, for they had been common enough in England; the colonists thought of them as warnings to slaves, though of course they were also warning and counseling themselves by erecting tangible monuments to their own fears.[117]

Our attention must focus on the message sent to the whites by such "monuments." The slaughter, torture, and public displays of the brutalized bodies of slaves and other "blacks" who rebelled served as a warning to all persons "black" or "white" who would not conform to white, upper-class authority that they would be swiftly and summarily dealt with.

Poor whites, Goad reminds us, got the message. "When all the horrors are peeled away," Goad pointedly notes, the "business [of stealing bodies] was precisely that — a business." Goad reiterates this point when noting that "[a]s with black slaves from Africa, white slaves from Europe were being kidnaped and shipped overseas not for reasons of unvarnished human hatred, but because it was profitable."[118]

As we saw in chapter 2, the European servile classes, early on, were afraid not of the Africans who labored beside them in the fields but, rather, of their common class overlords. Our point in recapitulating this history is basic: *the historically grounded fear in the white laboring classes of white, upper-class violence against them was symbolized by the tortured body of "blacks."*

As we saw in chapter 5, in the twentieth century George Wallace and other race politicians and pundits preyed on the white fears of black rebellion and black assault for the sake of vested political interests. This strategy was a way of addressing white fears. But an original source of these white fears remained inexplicable because the original problem was ignored by the masses and their so-called leaders: how to control rebellions against the white elite by both black and white members of the lower classes.

The answer, of course, was to create a "white" self-consciousness filled with a darkened self-contempt for lower-class weaknesses and vulnerabilities to upper-class interests.[119] Goad makes this point in his own personal tale when describing the way in which he learned to "disown [his] own roots" and feel shame.[120] Such self-contempt cannot be resolved by trying to look like a prosperous white.

A genuine resolution to this problem, however, is at hand. Our primer lets us identify and name the actual feelings of self-contempt engendered in persons who are forced to act "white" in order to survive in their own communities. We call these feelings *white shame*. Using this primer, we can affirm that such human feelings of shame do

- indicate the presence of a broken human spirit, a fallen human nature, a fracture to one's core ability to relate, and

- reveal that sin is indeed present.

Our explanations of these sinful feelings, however, have a critical social edge. In short, we take into account the social environment that creates "whites" and engenders feelings of "white" shame. We note the pervasive child abuse practices, racial indoctrination programs, and class exploitation strategies of Euro-American communities that impair their members' abilities to relate wholeheartedly to others. Our critical investigation thus helps us make sense of the pervasive racial and class fears found in so many Euro-Americans today: shame. They feel *white* shame because the persons who ostensibly loved and respected them the most actually abused them and justified it in the name of race, money, and God.

# EPILOGUE

The end of this book is a beginning, a place where new conversations about money, race, and God in America can commence.

With this new beginning, loyalties need no longer be skin-deep.

Here God's broken humanity can be healed.

Difference will be affirmed as the grace of human engagement.

The term *person of color* will now refer to every human being.

Dare we dream of such a day?

Yes.

Let the church say Amen.

# NOTES

## Chapter 1: White

1. As labor historian David Roediger notes in his book *Towards the Abolition of Whiteness* (London: Verso, 1994), discussions of "race" in America usually mean talk about "African Americans, Native Americans, Hispanic Americans, and Asian Americans. If whites come into the discussion, it is only because they have 'attitudes towards nonwhites'" (12).

2. I use pseudonyms throughout this presentation. For some of the more confessional stories, I have also changed the city in which the story was told to me to further protect the identity of the speaker.

3. Antiracist Lutheran minister and author Joseph Barndt, for example, claims in the introduction to his book *Dismantling Racism: The Continuing Challenge to White America* (Minneapolis: Augsburg, 1991) that his goal is to "help white people understand how racism functions and is perpetuated in our homes, schools, churches, and other institutions" so that they can "combat and dismantle racism" and build a multiracial, multicultural society (5). For Barndt, the most basic problem whites have to address is racism. My approach begins elsewhere. I am interested in one way in which the Euro-American child learns to think of itself as white. It learns to do so as a self-protection against racial abuse from its own community.

4. Dana Crowley Jack, *Silencing the Self: Women and Depression* (New York: HarperPerennial, 1991), 137–38.

5. Two important studies on race awareness in young children are particularly worth noting here: anthropologist Mary Ellen Goodman's *Race Awareness in Young Children* (New York: Collier Books, 1962); and psychologist William E. Cross Jr.'s *Shades of Black: Diversity in African-American Identity* (Philadelphia: Temple University Press, 1991).

6. Heinz Kohut, the founder of self-psychology, argues in *The Search for the Self: Selected Writings of Heinz Kohut: 1950–1978*, vol. 2, ed. Paul H. Ornstein (New York: International Universities Press, 1978), 615–58, that the parts of the self that are consistently not lovingly and empathically mirrored and thus affirmed are split off from the child's operative conscious activities of engagement with self and others (this operative consciousness is also referred to as "the reality ego") or are separated from the self through repression. This "split-off sector of the psyche" is not, however, the end of the story. Occasionally, these fulsome feelings of unrequited empathic engagement and bonding bypass the repression barrier constructed by the child's reality ego or break through

the brittle defenses, thus overwhelming and flooding the ego with unmoderated feelings. Overwhelmed, the ego is momentarily paralyzed.

When this occurs, the child simultaneously experiences intense shame because of the release of proscribed feelings. Rage is also felt because the child's original feelings were frustrated when its caretaking milieu required the child to split off its own unmet needs from consciousness in order to survive in a toxic caretaking environment.

The blush, according to Kohut, is thus a kind of "temporary paralysis" in which the ego both yields to the pressure to exhibit the outpouring from the split-off sector of the self and at the same time desperately attempts to stem the tide. This conflictual process can be thought of as a self's psychological civil war. Each of us is occasionally embroiled in such internal skirmishes. We all blush or perspire or in some way demonstrate an acutely embarrassing physical expression of momentary internal skirmishes to stave off proscribed feelings that have overwhelmed us. Kohut proffers a precise psychological description of blushing as an indication of the internal civil war called shame: "The exhibitionistic surface of the body-self, the skin, ... shows ... heat and blushing side by side with pallor. It is this disorganized mixture of massive discharge (tension decrease) and blockage (tension increase) in the area of exhibitionistic libido that is experienced as shame" (655).

7. Léon Wurmser, *The Mask of Shame* (Northvale, N.J.: Jason Aronson, 1997), 93. Wurmser's own theory of shame emphasizes psychoanalytic drive and affect theory. Wurmser believes that Kohut's self-psychology diminishes the role of conflicts and defenses in his psychoanalytic explanation of shame.

8. Kohut, *Search for the Self*, 615–58.

9. Helen Merrell Lynd, *On Shame and the Search for Identity* (New York: Harcourt, Brace and Company, 1958), chap. 2, "The Nature of Shame," 27–71.

10. Ibid.

11. Donald L. Nathanson, *Shame and Pride: Affect, Sex, and the Birth of the Self* (New York: W. W. Norton, 1992). A fine summary of the field of shame theory can be found in Robert Karen's "Shame," *Atlantic Monthly* (February 1992).

12. Lynd, *On Shame.*

13. Based on my own informal survey among friends and workshop participants, I cannot determine how often such feelings of unlovability reside behind the term *white*. That this pattern is pervasive I have no doubt. How pervasive awaits determination by social-scientific surveys designed to determine the extent of this pattern. I simply remain amazed to this day that virtually every adult Euro-American I have talked with can give me an example from her or his own life to corroborate this feeling of shame brought on by early experiences that prompted that person to form her or his white identity. Is my theory a self-fulfilling prophecy, defining what it identifies? I doubt it because I discovered this pattern before I had a theory to explain it.

14. Wurmser, *Mask of Shame*, 93.

15. Gordon W. Allport, *The Nature of Prejudice* (Reading, Mass.: Addison-Wesley, 1979), 29.

16. Ibid., 39.

17. Ibid., 297.

18. Andrew P. Morrison, *The Culture of Shame* (New York: Ballantine Books, 1996).

19. Ibid., 119.

20. The term *not-quite-good-enough* is used by pediatrician and psychoanalytic theorist D. W. Winnicott to describe the failed emotional environment that both splits the child's sense of itself and exploits the way in which it thinks about itself and others. See Winnicott's essay "Thinking and Symbolic Formation," in *Psychoanalytic Explorations,* ed. Clare Winnicott, Ray Shepherd, and Madeleine Davis (Cambridge, Mass.: Harvard University Press, 1989), 213–16.

21. Alice Miller, *Prisoners of Childhood: The Drama of the Gifted Child and the Search for the True Self,* trans. Ruth Ward (New York: Basic Books, 1981), 6, 12.

## Chapter 2: Abuse

1. Wallace's motive for writing this essay is to document a Southern California police force out of control when issues of race-mixing are involved. By so doing, he intends to focus white attention on the activities of the Los Angeles police force that might have led the jurors of O. J. Simpson's murder trial to acquit him. Police misconduct (because of Simpson's white wife) rather than juror racial loyalty, Wallace wishes to argue, might explain Simpson's "swift acquittal." To accomplish this task, Wallace recounts personal incidents of how "[t]his white boy got the message long ago" that race-mixing is forbidden.

2. Wallace never tells the reader why he and his family were on Olvera Street. One senses, however, that they were there to enjoy and appreciate "old California's Mexican heritage."

3. Mary Ellen Goodman, *Race Awareness in Young Children* (New York: Collier Books, 1964 [1952]), 47.

4. As anthropologist Mary Ellen Goodman notes in *Race Awareness in Young Children,* her classic study of 103 four-year-olds, a fourth of the children had already developed positive and negative racial values such as hatred toward black persons and not liking brown faces. For these children, "their systems of race-related values are strongly entrenched" (47). The rest of the children had a racial attitude that made them ready to adopt a race-related value system once they learned a word like *nigger* from the older children (48).

5. My brief summary of presymbolic patterning principles of interaction between child and caretaker that can establish the patterns for later symbolic forms is based on the fine analysis of the patterns of interactions between mother and infant as a basis for the child's emerging symbolic forms by psychoanalytic theorists Beatrice Beebe and Frank M. Lachmann in their essay "The Contribution of Mother-Infant Mutual Influence to the Origins of Self and Object Representation," in *Relational Perspectives in Psychoanalysis,* ed. Neil J. Skolnick and Susan C. Warshal (Hillsdale, N.J.: Analytic Press, 1992), 83–117.

6. Ibid., 47–48.

7. Frantz Fanon, *Black Skin, White Masks,* trans. Charles Lam Markmann (New York: Grove Press, 1967), 112.

8. Ibid., 113.

9. See Raymond Massey and Nancy Denton, *American Apartheid: Segregation and the Creation of the Underclass in America* (Cambridge, Mass.: Harvard University Press, 1993), for a detailed sociological study of the way in which the black ghettos were created and are maintained in America. Architect and theorist Leslie Kanes Weisman also provides a vivid account of the covenant codes, government strategies, zoning practices, and business agendas that systematically created racial ghettos in America. See Weisman's *Discrimination by Design: A Feminist Critique of the Man-Made Environment* (Urbana: University of Illinois Press, 1992).

10. From this subjective perspective, we can thus both affirm and qualify the claim by sociologist Howard Winant that "whiteness is a relational concept, unintelligible without reference to nonwhiteness" (Winant, "Behind Blue Eyes: Whiteness and Contemporary U.S. Racial Politics," in *Off White: Readings on Race, Power, and Society,* ed. Michelle Fine et al. [New York: Routledge: 1997], 48). The nonwhiteness of whiteness does not necessarily refer to another person from a nonwhite racial group. Rather, this nonwhiteness can simply be the feeling of a person with a white racial identity that cannot be factored into consciousness and affirmed as a personal desire. Such feelings, as we saw in chapter 1, are often masked and expressed as blackened desires.

11. D. W. Winnicott, "Marion Milner: Critical Notice of *On Not Being Able to Paint,*" in *Psychoanalytic Explorations,* ed. Clare Winnicott, Ray Shepperd, and Madeleine Davis (Cambridge, Mass.: Harvard University Press, 1989), 390.

12. Flannery O'Connor, "The Artificial Nigger," in *The Complete Stories* (New York: Noonday Press and Farrar, Straus and Giroux, 1972), 262.

13. In this definition I have used psychoanalytic theorist D. W. Winnicott's notion of the false self as "a defensive organization in which there is a premature taking over of the nursing functions of the mother, so that the infant or child adapts to the environment while at the same time protecting and hiding the true self, or the source of personal impulses" (Winnicott, "Ideas and Definitions," in *Psychoanalytic Explorations,* 43).

14. Gordon W. Allport, *The Nature of Prejudice* (Reading, Mass.: Addison-Wesley, 1979), 322.

15. Andrew P. Morrison, *The Culture of Shame* (New York: Ballantine Books, 1996), 149.

16. Ibid., 150. Morrison, however, does not investigate the shaming experience entailed in becoming white. Rather, race for Morrison pertains to "racism" and the "racism-poverty-shame shackle" found in black America's urban ghettos. General discussions that link race and shame, for Morrison, pertain to "black" shame and "institutional oppression."

Accordingly, when Morrison lists the "various guises" that can conceal shame, such as rage, contempt, envy, and depression, he overlooks the guise of whiteness as a self-degrading system of identify formation (132). This oversight leads him to miss a major element at play in his discussion of violence. Morrison rightly suggests that violence is a possible outcome of a society's failure to address or redress the inequities and humiliations within its purview (198). By overlooking the shame entailed in becoming white but not being WASP in America, Morrison ignores the intraracial violence within white America that spills over into the rest of America as the appearance of white racism, white pride, and white bigotry. Much of this white violence flows from the racial rage attached to white racial shame. As Morrison notes, if there is a major discrepancy between the " 'desired' self (perfect, all-competent, etc.) and the self-as-experienced for a given patient, core shame is likely to be of central importance" (163).

My point is that the core shame of white "ethnicity" needs to be systematically addressed as an example of white shame entailed in acquiring and maintaining a white racial identity in America. This core problem will not be systematically addressed, however, until it is seen. This requires that Euro-American psychoanalysts turn their own eyes inward. To understand the nature of the ethnic white rage that Podhoretz's attitudes toward the African American display, the Euro-American psychoanalyst must first explore the nature and structure of his or her own white shame.

Indeed Morrison himself suggests in his essay "The Eye Turned Inward: Shame and the Self" (in *The Many Faces of Shame*, ed. Donald L. Nathanson [New York: Guilford Press, 1987]) that if therapists have not dealt with their own participation in "the shaming systems of everyday life," they will be unable to adequately cope with the shaming experiences of their clients (290). Morrison's perspective thus provides an optimal context for taking into consideration the issue of *white* shame in the formation of an ethnic white identity. The therapist, Morrison argues, must "make a practice of facing and learning about his or her *own* shame experiences, his or her own lack of self-acceptance" (290). This self-attention will lead inevitably to the shaming experiences of the patient. Morrison can make this claim because his shame theory focuses on the "eye of the self gazing inwards." What is required is that this eye pay attention to its own race issues entailed in becoming "a white" (273). A shame theory and a theory about becoming white are both required for an adequate assessment from a psychoanalytic standpoint of the "culture of shame" Morrison finds so pervasive in America today.

17. Morrison, *Culture of Shame*, 132.

18. Norman Podhoretz, *Making It* (New York: Random House, 1967), 67–68.

19. Norman Podhoretz, *Breaking Ranks: A Political Memoir* (New York: Harper and Row, 1979).

20. Norman Podhoretz, "My Negro Problem — and Ours," *Commentary* (February 1963): 93.

21. Podhoretz, *Making It*, 12–14.

22. Ibid., 27.

23. Sander L. Gilman, *Jewish Self-Hatred: Anti-Semitism and the Hidden Language of the Jews* (Baltimore: Johns Hopkins University Press, 1986), 8–10.

24. Sander L. Gilman, *Freud, Race, and Gender* (Princeton, N.J.: Princeton University Press, 1993), 19.

25. Podhoretz, "My Negro Problem," 93–101

26. As Robert Jay Lifton notes in his book *The Broken Connection: On Death and the Continuity of Life* (New York: Simon and Schuster, 1979), thwarted efforts at personal integration and self-definition produce a loss of self-integrity that feels like an inner death. The impulse to stave off such death threats to the self are violent because the self is fighting for its life. This relationship of threatened inner death and violent impulse is central to the experiential continuum of anger-rage-violence. The intensity of the response depends upon the intensity of the feeling of inner threat (149). I would like to thank psychoanalytic theorist Michael Flynn for recommending Lifton's book to me for its analysis of this link between the collapse of the self and violence impulses.

27. Ibid., 100.

28. Léon Wurmser, *The Mask of Shame* (Northvale, N.J.: Jason Aronson, 1995), 302, 69.

29. Psychoanalytic theorist Léon Wurmser uses the image of the mask to fine effect in *The Mask of Shame*. Masks, as Wurmser notes, have been associated by the Swiss ethnologist Karl Meuli with cults of the dead and the presence of the spirits of deceased ancestors. The Old High German root term for shame — *scama* — means "to cover one's self." The modern German word means "shadow" or "ghost." This association between covering and ghost, and between the meaning of shame and the wearing of masks, leads Wurmser to play with the ideas of shame, death, and hiding. For Wurmser there is an "archetypal relation" between the mask and shame. On the one hand, by wearing a mask, one can identify with what horrifies one by turning the death of oneself into a spirit that calls for revenge. Or, on the other hand, one can ridicule and laugh at the hidden shame through minstrelling (304–5).

We have only to think of the white mask of the Klansman and the blackface minstrel shows of white workers to grasp the immediate relevancy of Wurmser's reflections to our present discussion of *white* shame. Behind the white mask lies the phobic content of the other who is as close to the self as the I. Shame, as Wurmser notes, takes cover. It disguises itself as expressions of rage, contempt, and envy. This hiding of shame is the shame of shame — the self caught in the throes of its own civil war.

30. This latter interpretation of Podhoretz's "insane rage" against black anti-Semitism was suggested to me by David Reich, the editor of *World* magazine. From this vantage point, the issue of ethnic shame remains as the problem of not being a more highly esteemed white because of one's low ethnic ranking. Podhoretz would thus feel rage toward Negro anti-Semites because they had exposed his own low racial status. Such exposures might result in feelings of ethnic shame. His rage, in short, would be a mask of his own feelings of racial shame.

31. Podhoretz, *Making It,* 61.

32. Donald L. Nathanson, *Shame and Pride: Affect, Sex, and the Birth of the Self* (New York: W. W. Norton, 1992), 200.

33. Ibid., 202.

34. Podhoretz, "My Negro Problem," 101.

35. Podhoretz, *Breaking Ranks,* 132.

36. This complex sideshow is reminiscent of the early white Alabama communists described by labor historian David Roediger in his essay "Gaining

a Hearing for Black-White Unity," in *Towards the Abolition of Whiteness* (London: Verso, 1994). These communists referred to black party members as "comrade nigger." Trying to make sense of this complex proposition by white, southern communists toward their black comrades, Roediger writes that "it is difficult to know if they did so out of habit, out of a need to reaffirm a sense of whiteness even as they broke racial taboos, out of a misplaced certainty that the power of the first of their words took all the sting from the second, or for all of these reasons at once" (148). See Robin D. G. Kelley, *Hammer and Hoe: Alabama Communists during the Great Depression* (Chapel Hill: University of North Carolina Press, 1990), 137, 28. Podhoretz's invitation to an imagined prospective black son-in-law is, at least, as complex an attitude.

37. Richard Sennett and Jonathan Cobb, *The Hidden Injuries of Class* (New York: W. W. Norton, 1972), 18–20.

38. Much to their credit, Sennett and Cobb freely acknowledge that the discovery of this self-accusatory terrain of shame within the workers interviewed was unexpected. This discovery, in fact, forced the scholars to set aside their own previous assumptions about the classical ways in which workers have been exploited and disempowered by a capitalist system. A Marxist perspective lacked the scope to explain the conundrum they had come upon. The workers, the scholars argued, reacted to power in "a much more complicated way" than a classic Marxist analysis could explain. Much to the chagrin of the two scholars, the workers accepted their own status as legitimate even though they also believed the division of America into the haves and have-nots is undignified in itself (ibid., 78).

39. Ibid. 97.

40. Ibid., 98, 73.

41. A vivid history of housing discrimination is given by sociologists Douglas S. Massey and Nancy A. Denton in their book *American Apartheid: Segregation and the Making of the Underclass* (Cambridge, Mass.: Harvard University Press, 1993).

42. Sennett and Cobb, *Hidden Injuries*, 81.

43. Ibid., 18.

44. Ibid., 17.


## Chapter 3: Class

1. Edmund S. Morgan, *American Slavery, American Freedom: The Ordeal of Colonial Virginia* (New York: W. W. Norton, 1975), 325.

2. Ibid., 327.

3. I have used the discussion of the links between shame and feelings of contempt and superiority found in the section of Susan Miller's book *The Shame Experience* (Hillsdale, N.J.: Analytic Press, 1993) titled "Interactions between Shame and Feelings of Superiority and Inferiority" (138–39).

4. Morgan, *American Slavery*, 144, 216, 96.

5. Ibid. As Morgan notes, "There had always been in Virginia a rough congruity of Christianity, whiteness, and freedom and of heathenism, non-

whiteness, and slavery. The early acts defining the servitude of Negroes and Indians had assumed that they would both normally be non-Christian" (331).

6. Ibid., 329–33.

7. Ibid., 338–47. In early sections of his book, Morgan chronicles the Virginians' equally virulent attitudes and behavior toward the "heathen savages" of North America. For a fine historical overview and analysis of the ways in which the early Euro-Americans' changing attitudes toward Native Americans — attitudes shaped by economic interests and land acquisition — functioned as a formative ground for the construction of racial attitudes toward Africans and African Americans, see Gary B. Nash, "Red, White and Black: The Origins of Racism in Colonial America," in *The Great Fear: Race in the Mind of America*, ed. Gary B. Nash and Richard Weiss (New York: Holt, Rinehart and Winston, 1970), 1–26.

8. Morgan, *American Slavery*, 338.

9. Ibid., 326. As Morgan notes, "[The poor] were not only troublesome, but also 'nauseous to the Beholders.'... [T]hey could be segregated, along with other vicious, insane, diseased, or impotent persons within the walls of the workhouses, hospitals, prisons, and asylums constructed to enclose them — the ghettos of the poor — or else they could be shipped to the plantations and contribute their share to the national income there." The phrase "nauseous to the Beholders" is taken from John Cary's book *A Discourse on Trade* (London, 1745), 121.

10. Ann Laura Stoler, *Race and the Education of Desire: Foucault's History of Sexuality and the Colonial Order of Things* (Durham, N.C.: Duke University Press, 1995), especially chap. 4, "Cultivating Bourgeois Bodies and Racial Selves," 95–136.

11. Morgan, *American Slavery*, 327.

12. Theodore W. Allen, *The Invention of the White Race: The Origin of Racial Oppression in Anglo-America*, vol. 2 (London: Verso, 1997), 231. See also *Acts of Assembly Passed in the Island of Nevis from 1664 to 1739 Inclusive*, 35–39.

13. Morgan, *American Slavery*, 295–315. The details of my discussion of profit are taken from this chapter, entitled "Toward Slavery."

14. Ibid., 299–315.

15. Ibid., chaps. 15, "Toward Slavery," and 16, "Toward Racism," 316–37.

16. Ibid., 308, 217.

17. Ibid., 215–92, 327.

18. Ibid., 309.

19. Ibid., 328.

20. Theodore W. Allen, *The Invention of the White Race: The Origin of Racial Oppression in Anglo-America*, vol. 1 (London: Verso, 1994), 137–38.

21. Ibid., 138. Allen cites Great Britain Public Record Office, *Calendar of State Papers, Colonial*, 7:141 (December 14, 1670); and *Colonial Records of the State of Georgia*, 1:58, for further discussion of these penal laws.

22. As Morgan notes, "It would be difficult to argue that the introduction of slavery brought direct economic benefits to free labor in Virginia" (*American Slavery*, 344).

23. Ibid., 341. Class distinctions were neither eliminated nor lessened. Rather, the conditions of the members within these groups were modified.

24. Allen, *Invention,* vols. 1 and 2.

25. Allen, *Invention,* 1:137n.9. See also vol. 2 of Allen's work.

26. A. Leon Higginbotham Jr., *Shades of Freedom: Racial Politics and Presumptions of the American Legal System* (New York: Oxford University Press, 1996), 4.

27. Ibid., xxv.

28. Morgan, *American Slavery,* 335. See H. R. McIlwaine, ed., *Legislative Journals of the Council of Colonial Virginia* (Richmond, 1918), 1:262.

29. Manuscript, Court Records of Elizabeth City County, 1684–99, 27 and 83, in Virginia State Library (cited by John H. Russell, *The Free Negro in Virginia: 1619–1865* [New York: Dover Publications, 1969], 124–25).

30. Russell, *Free Negro,* 298.

31. Ibid., 125–28.

32. Ibid., 149.

33. Ibid., 147. See manuscripts of petitions, Henrico County, 1825, A 9358, A 9359.

34. Russell, *Free Negro,* 147. See *House Journal,* 1847–48, p. 20. As Russell further notes, "Governor Smith reaffirmed this belief in his message of 1848" (ibid., 1848–49, p. 22).

35. Russell notes that by the nineteenth century, there were "tens of thousands" of free Negroes in Virginia (ibid., 126).

36. Ibid., 147–48. See message, in *House Journal,* 1848–49, p. 22 and 1847–48, p. 20.

37. Russell, *Free Negro,* 13.

38. Ibid., 12.

39. Ibid., 26 (cited by Du Bois from Frederick L. Olmstead, *A Journey in the Seaboard Slave States* [1856], 404).

40. W. E. B. Du Bois, *Black Reconstruction in America: 1860–1880* (1935; reprint, Cleveland: Meridian Books, 1964), 32–33.

41. Ibid., 26. See also Herman Schlueter, *Lincoln, Labor and Slavery* (1913), 86.

42. As Orville Vernon Burton notes in his essay "The Burden of Southern Historiography: W. J. Cash and the Old South," in *The Mind of the South: Fifty Years Later,* ed. Charles W. Eagles (Jackson: University Press of Mississippi, 1992): "Historians are currently taking another serious look at the man whose book has remained important, whether as interpreter or straw man, for references to the American South. In fact, in this golden anniversary year, Cash is hot! A new biography, papers or sessions at several historical associations, and at least two conferences are devoted to Cash" (60–61).

43. Cash, *The Mind of the South* (New York: Alfred A. Knopf, 1941), 58.

44. Ibid., 68–69.

45. Ibid., 41.

46. Ibid., 39.

47. Ibid., 110.

48. Ibid., 61.

49. Ibid., 43.

50. Ibid., 49–50.

51. Frantz Fanon, *Black Skin, White Masks,* trans. Charles Lam Markmann (New York: Grove Press, 1967).

52. Ibid., 48–49.

53. Ibid., 84.

54. Burton, "W. J. Cash and the Old South," 62, 71; see also Michael O'Brien, "Commentary," in *The Mind of the South.* O'Brien writes: "The various conferences held this year have made the fact abundantly clear, that Wilbur Cash has almost nothing to say to blacks and women. For them, he is part of the problem of Southern culture" (56).

55. James Baldwin, *Notes of a Native Son* (Boston: Beacon Press, 1984), 25.


*Chapter 4: Loss*

1. Eric Lott, *Love and Theft: Blackface Minstrelsy and the American Working Class* (New York: Oxford University Press, 1993), 53.

2. Robert T. Toll, *Blacking Up: The Minstrel Show in Nineteenth-Century America* (New York: Oxford University Press, 1974), 67.

3. Ibid., 67–68.

4. Lott, *Love and Theft,* 161–62. The quotation cited by Lott is from Olive Logan, "Ancestry of Brudder Bones," *Harper's New Monthly Magazine* 58, no. 347 (1879): 698.

5. Toll, *Blacking Up,* 67.

6. Ibid., 72–73. Toll cites "Nigga's Heart Am Bery Gay," in *Negro Melodist* (Cincinnati, 1850[?]), 47–48; and Charles White, "We'll All Make a Laugh," in *New Book of Plantation Melodies,* 12; among others.

7. David Roediger, *The Wages of Whiteness: Race and the Making of the American Working Class* (London: Verso, 1991), 117.

8. Ibid.

9. Toll, *Blacking Up,* 25–31.

10. Ibid., 31.

11. Ibid., 51–57.

12. Ibid., 12.

13. Cited by Lott, *Love and Theft,* 5.

14. Toll, *Blacking Up,* 10–11.

15. Ibid., 16.

16. Ibid., 16–17.

17. Ibid.

18. Herbert G. Gutman with Ira Berlin, "Class Composition and the Development of the American Working Class, 1840–1890," in *Power and Culture: Essays on the American Working Class,* ed. Ira Berlin (New York: Pantheon Books, 1987), 383–84.

19. Gutman and Berlin also counted American "blacks" as part of the 75 percent or more of nineteenth-century workers who were not native-born Euro-Americans. As they note in summarizing their findings, "[W]ith a few ex-

ceptions, after 1840 most American workers were immigrants or the children of immigrants" (ibid., 385).

20. Ibid., 380.

21. George P. Rawick, *From Sundown to Sunup: The Making of the Black Community* (Westport, Conn.: Greenwood Publishing Co., 1972).

22. Herbert G. Gutman, *Work, Culture, and Society in Industrializing America* (New York: Vintage Books, 1976), 19.

23. Ibid., 20–21.

24. Ibid., 22.

25. Ibid., 33–34. To emphasize this point Gutman cites Edward P. Thompson's masterful study, *The Making of the English Working Class* (London, 1963). Thompson writes that "alternative bouts of intense labour and of idleness [occurred] whenever men were in control of their working lives."

26. Ibid., 38. Gutman cites the observations of a ship carpenter who described these self-imposed relaxation periods as "an indulgence that custom had made as much of a necessity in a New York shipyard as a grind-stone."

27. Ibid., 39.

28. Ibid., 41.

29. Ibid., 44–45.

30. Ibid., 43.

31. Toll, *Blacking Up*, 181

32. Ibid., 179.

33. Roediger, *Wages of Whiteness*, 58. See also Philip S. Foner and Ronald L. Lewis, eds., *The Black Worker: A Documentary History from Colonial Times to the Present* (Philadelphia: Temple University Press, 1978), 1:175–77.

34. Roediger, *Wages of Whiteness*, 58.

35. Gutman, *Work, Culture, and Society*, 71–72.

36. William Isaac Thomas, Robert E. Park, and Herbert A. Miller, *Old World Traits Transplanted* (1921; reprint, Montclair, N.J.: Patterson Smith, 1971), 281. This text was brought to my attention by a reference in Gutman's *Work, Culture, and Society*, 73.

37. Thomas, Park, and Miller, *Old World Traits Transplanted*, 303.

38. Ibid., 272–73.

39. Gutman, *Power and Culture*, 400, citing the words of a Lowell, Massachusetts, clergyman in 1845.

40. Ibid., 400.

41. Thomas, Park, and Miller, *Old World Traits Transplanted*, 92–93.

42. Ibid., 280.

43. Susan Miller, *The Shame Experience* (Hillsdale, N.J.: Analytic Press, 1993), 134.

44. Ibid., 124.

45. Frederick Douglass, *North Star* (newspaper), October 27, 1848; cited by Lott, *Love and Theft*, 15.

46. Alexander Saxton, "Blackface Minstrelsy and Jacksonian Ideology," *American Quarterly* 27, no. 1 (1975): 27; cited by Lott, *Love and Theft*, 3.

47. Martin Mayman offers this fine summary of affect and Freud's discussion of its role in psychoanalysis. Mayman's comments are in his foreword to Miller, *Shame Experience*, xii–xiii.

48. Ibid.

49. Lott, *Love and Theft*, 162.

50. Ibid., 163–64.

51. Lott, *Love and Theft*, 53. In this citation, Lott uses passages from Willie Morris's *North toward Home* (Boston: Houghton Mifflin, 1967), 81; and Leslie A. Fiedler's *Waiting for the End* (New York: Stein and Day, 1972), 134.

52. Norman Podhoretz, "My Negro Problem — and Ours," *Commentary* (February 1963): 93–101.

53. Lott, *Love and Theft*, 271.


## Chapter 5: Victims

1. Labor historian David R. Roediger, in his book *The Wages of Whiteness: Race and the Making of the American Working Class* (London: Verso, 1991), presents a fine account of the value Euro-American workers believed they accrued by distinguishing themselves through *whiteness* as free rather than slave labor (13–14). Roediger's work first brought to my attention W. E. B. Du Bois's description of "a sort of public and psychological wage" given to whites to compensate for their low wages. See Du Bois's *Black Reconstruction in America: 1860–1880* (1935; reprint, Cleveland: Meridian Books, 1964), 700.

2. Du Bois, *Black Reconstruction*, 701–2.

3. Ibid., 700.

4. Ibid., 26–27.

5. Ibid., 28.

6. Ibid., 701.

7. Ibid.

8. Cheryl I. Harris, "Whiteness as Property," *Harvard Law Review* 106 (1993): 1759.

9. Ibid., 1758. As Harris notes, this prize made sure that the value of whiteness was retained: "[I]t does not mean that all whites will win, but simply that they will not lose." Harris refers to the work of Andrew Hacker in his book *Two Nations: Black and White, Separate, Hostile and Unequal* (1992), 29, as the source of this keen insight.

10. Susan Miller, *The Shame Experience* (Hillsdale, N.J.: Analytic Press, 1993), 33. As Miller notes, "[T]he sense of the self as diminished [is] the core of what I am calling the shame experience."

11. Martin Luther King Jr., *Where Do We Go from Here: Chaos or Community?* (Boston: Beacon Press, 1967), 7–8.

12. Ibid.

13. Ibid., 152.

14. David J. Garrow, *The FBI and Martin Luther King, Jr.* (New York: W. W. Norton, 1981), 214–15, 183.

15. Martin Luther King Jr., *The Trumpet of Conscience* (New York: Harper and Row, 1967), 59–60.

16. Garrow, *FBI*, 214; Garrow here references an unpublished manuscript.

17. Cited in ibid.

18. King, *Where Do We Go*, 186.

19. Ibid., 5.

20. Ibid., 8.

21. Ibid., 139.

22. Ibid., 68, 83.

23. David J. Garrow, *Bearing the Cross: Martin Luther King, Jr., ana the Southern Christian Leadership Conference* (New York: Vintage Books, 1988), 500.

24. Ibid., 536–37.

25. Martin Luther King Jr., "Pilgrimage to Nonviolence," in *Strength to Love* (New York: Pocket Books, 1963), 170; see also "Loving Your Enemies" in the same book.

26. King, "Pilgrimage to Nonviolence," 170.

27. Martin Luther King Jr., *A Testament of Hope: The Essential Writings and Speeches of Martin Luther King, Jr.*, ed. James M. Washington (San Francisco: HarperSanFrancisco, 1986), 75.

28. King's oversight is unsurprising. In fact, he shared this perspective with the Swedish economist, social scientist, and diplomat Gunnar Myrdal, who, in his classic 1944 study of white attitudes toward Negroes, *An American Dilemma*, vol. 2: *The Negro Problem and Modern Democracy* (1944; reprint, New Brunswick: Transaction Publishers, 1996), identified a "split in [the white American's] moral personality" (1003). A decade before King began his civil rights work, Myrdal suggested that the gap between white Americans' personal belief in democracy and their actual treatment of Negroes would trouble their conscience as Negro protests became more numerous. This would happen, Myrdal argued, because "[p]eople want to be rational, and they want to feel that they are good and righteous" (1003). Mounting Negro protest would thus not only reveal the incongruity between what whites say and what they do but also bring on a moral crisis in America's civic soul. King was bearing out Myrdal's prediction when he strove to bring this white American "moral dilemma" out into the open by targeting the white conscience.

29. King, "Pilgrimage to Nonviolence," 170.

30. King, "Loving Your Enemies," 43.

31. King, *Where Do We Go*, 74–75.

32. Ibid., 72.

33. Miller, *Shame Experience*.

34. Winthrop D. Jordan, *The White Man's Burden: Historical Origins of Racism in the United States* (London: Oxford University Press, 1974), 61–62.

35. Ian F. Haney Lopez, *White by Law: The Legal Construction of Race* (New York: New York University Press, 1996), 19.

36. Ibid., 17.

37. To make this point, Lopez focuses on thirty-seven of fifty-two such racial prerequisite cases, two of which were heard by the U.S. Supreme Court (ibid., 4, 32).

38. Ibid., chapter 2, "Racial Restrictions in the Law of Citizenship," 37–47.

39. Leon F. Litwack, *North of Slavery: The Negro in the Free States 1790–1860* (Chicago: University of Chicago Press, 1961), 31.

40. Ibid., 31n. Litwack here cites the following references: *Appendix to the Annals of Congress*, 1 Cong., 2 sess., pp. 2205–6; 2 Congr., 1 sess., p. 1392; 11 Cong., 1 and 2 sess., p. 2569; 16 Cong., 1 sess., pp. 2600–2610; *Appendix to the Congressional Debates*, 18 Cong., 2 sess., p. 91.

41. Ibid. Litwack adds the following note to this statement: "After the admission of Maine in 1819, for example, every state that came into the Union before the end of the Civil War confined the suffrage to whites." Litwack refers to Charles H. Wesley, "Negro Suffrage in the Period of Constitution Making, 1787–1865," *Journal of Negro History* 32 (1947): 154.

42. Litwack, *North of Slavery*, 31–32. Litwack goes on to note that "consistency did not distinguish the actions of the national legislature. On one occasion it recognized — perhaps inadvertently — that Negroes might qualify as citizens. Against a background of increasing foreign difficulties, including the impressment of American seamen into the British navy, the House of Representatives resolved in 1803 'to enquire into the expediency of granting protection to such American seamen citizens of the United States, as are free persons of color' [*Journal of the House of Representatives*, 8 Cong., 1 sess., p. 224]." Litwack, however, also notes that "[t]en years later...Congress barred from employment on public or private vessels 'any person or persons except citizens of the United states, *or* persons of color, natives of the United States' [2 *U.S. Stat. At Large* 809]." Litwack concludes that "[p]rotecting the rights of Negro seamen in foreign waters apparently posed no threat to white supremacy at home."

43. Harris, "Whiteness as Property," 1725.

44. Ibid., 1766.

45. Ibid., 1725.

46. Ibid.

47. Lopez, *White by Law*, 15.

48. Barbara J. Flagg, " 'Was Blind, but Now I See': White Race Consciousness and the Requirement of Discriminatory Intent," *Michigan Law Review* 91 (1993): 969.

49. Ibid., 1017.

50. Ibid., 971.

51. This is the case because Flagg begins with a notion of the individual as an autonomous entity "analytically prior to that of society" (ibid., 953). Flagg's use of this traditional liberal notion of the individual's social identity as originally autonomous and discrete from its social environment prevents her from understanding the harrowing socialization process prior to one's conscious self-definition as a "white" that makes the retention of this racial designation in consciousness unendurable.

52. Ibid., 971.

53. Ibid.

54. Psychoanalytic theorist Judith Lewis Herman, in her book *Trauma and Recovery* (New York: Basic Books, 1992), has suggested that "[t]he ordinary response to atrocities is to banish them from consciousness. Certain violations of the social compact are too terrible to utter aloud: this is the meaning of the word *unspeakable*" (1). *White* is an unspeakable racial term, I am arguing, because this personal racial identity is the product of one's own community's assault upon one's personhood.

55. King, *Where Do We Go*, 137–38.

56. Garrow, *Bearing the Cross*, 617; cited from an interview with William A. Rutherford conducted by Garrow on February 25, 1982, in Washington, D.C.

57. Dan T. Carter, *The Politics of Rage: George Wallace, the Origins of the New Conservatism, and the Transformation of American Politics* (Baton Rouge: Louisiana State University Press, 1995), 207. Quotations from Wallace are taken from his Wisconsin Speech (see Alabama Department of Archives and History, Speech Collection [hereafter referred to as ADAHSC] [Montgomery, Alabama], and *Milwaukee Journal*, April 2, 1964).

58. Carter, *Politics of Rage*, 346. The statements by Hunter Thompson are taken from his book *Fear and Loathing on the Campaign Trail '72* (San Francisco: Straight Arrow Books, 1973), 156.

59. Carter, *Politics of Rage*, 208.

60. Ibid. Description of Wallace taken from the *New York Times*, April 9, 1963.

61. Carter, *Politics of Rage*, 161. Citations taken from "Speech by George C. Wallace... before the South Carolina Broadcasters Association, July 15, 1963" (ADAHSC); *Charleston News and Courier*, July 16, 1963; *The State* (Columbia, S.C.), July 16, 1963; emphasis added.

62. Carter, *Politics of Rage*, 293. This observation was made by Virginia Durr, in a letter to her friend Clark Foreman (letter from Durr to Clark Foreman, May 13, 1966, in Durr Papers, Radcliffe University Library; letter from Durr to Hugo Black, September 23, 1965, Black Papers, Library of Congress).

63. Carter, *Politics of Rage*, 293. Citation taken from Marshall Frady's book *Wallace*, 2d ed. (New York: New American Library, 1976). Carter notes that "Frady identifies the speaker simply as an 'Alabama judge,' but it is clearly Mayhall who publicly used the same remark (minus the profanity) in a speech the following year (*Birmingham News*, November 28, 1967)."

64. Carter, *Politics of Rage*, 293.

65. Carter cites a conversation with John Kohn on January 12, 1988, to this effect: "'If George had parachuted into the Albanian countryside in the spring of 1962,' said his former adviser John Kohn, 'he would have been head of a collective farm by the fall, a member of the Communist Party by mid-winter, on his way to the district party meeting as a delegate by the following year, and a member of the Comintern in two or three years. Hell,' he concluded, 'George could believe whatever he needed to believe'" (Carter, *Politics of Rage*, 15).

66. Ibid., 348–49. Nixon's statement to his staff members is taken from John Ehrlichman, *Witness to Power* (New York: Simon and Schuster, 1982), 223. Carter's immediate framework for this discussion is his reference to Nixon's

attempt to play "catch-up" to Wallace's talk of crime as a way to address white fears of a black threat. The citation for this discussion is taken from Joe McGinnis, *Selling of the President, 1968* (New York: Trident Press, 1969), 23.

67. The quotation is taken from Thomas F. Pettigrew and R. W. Meertens, "Subtle and Blatant Prejudice in Western Europe," *European Journal of Social Psychology* 25 (1995): 58. This quotation is found in Donald R. Kinder and Lynn M. Sanders, *Divided by Color: Racial Politics and Democratic Ideals* (Chicago: University of Chicago Press, 1996), 292. Kinder and Sanders note that "[a]ccording to Pettigrew and Meertens, subtle racism is composed of three elements: defense of traditional values, exaggeration of cultural — not genetic — differences, and denial or absence of positive emotional reactions, such as sympathy or admiration. The three are drawn together by a common thread, 'the socially acceptable rejection of minorities for ostensibly non-prejudicial reasons.'"

68. Kinder and Sanders, *Divided by Color,* 125.

69. Ibid., 268–69.

70. Ibid., 88.

71. Thomas Byrne Edsall and Mary D. Edsall, *Chain Reaction: The Impact of Race, Rights, and Taxes on American Politics* (New York: W. W. Norton, 1991), 11.

72. Michael Lind, *Up from Conservatism: Why the Right Is Wrong for America* (New York: Free Press Paperbacks, 1996).

73. Robert H. Bork, *Slouching towards Gomorrah: Modern Liberalism and the American Decline* (New York: Regan Books, 1996), chapter 12, "The Dilemmas of Race."

74. Ibid., 21.

75. Bork's view of the role and function of civil society, in this regard, is in keeping with the political philosophy of Thomas Hobbes, whose own dreary views of human nature led him to view the life of man outside the constraints of a civil state as "solitary, poor, nasty, brutish and short" (*Leviathan: Or the Matter, Forme and Power of a Commonwealth, Ecclesiastical and Civil* [New York: Collier Books, 1972], 100).

76. Bork, *Slouching towards Gomorrah,* 40.

77. Ibid., 40.

78. Ibid., 332, 74–76.

79. Ibid., 32.

80. Ibid., 25.

81. Ibid., 26–27.

82. Ibid., 27–35.

83. Ibid., 26.

84. Ibid., 26, 63–65, 75–77, and passim.

85. Ibid., 34, 63.

86. Ibid., 63.

87. Ibid., 235.

88. Ibid., chapter 12, "The Dilemmas of Race."

89. Ibid., 247.

90. Ibid., 237.

91. Bork plays the devil's advocate and assumes for a moment that such structural problems do exist. The position would nevertheless fail, Bork contends, because there are "laws upon laws forbidding discrimination in employment and promotion, in housing, in voting, in access to places of public accommodation, in lending, and much more. We have the Civil Rights Acts of 1866, 1871, 1964, 1968, and 1991; we have the Voting Rights Acts of 1965, 1975, and 1982. There is agency upon agency devoted to finding and ending discrimination: the Civil Rights Division of the Department of Justice, the Equal Employment Opportunity Commission, the Office of Federal Contract Compliance Programs, the Department of Education's Civil Rights Office, civil rights sections in various government agencies. There are thousands of such agencies, and more than 100,000 government lawyers, investigators, and agents who spend hundreds of millions of dollars enforcing the laws and regulations. If that were not enough, there are laws providing for private lawsuits and an army of private attorneys bringing discrimination claims. If discrimination is provable, we have far more than adequate means of dealing with it" (ibid., 235–36).

An opponent of Bork's position would simply say, "Where there is so much smoke..." Judge A. Leon Higginbotham, for example, might use this list as evidence to support his claim that the American legal process plays a major role in "substantiating, perpetuating, and legitimizing the precept of [black] inferiority." So many agencies and attorneys are needed because of the very structure of the legal beast: the use of law to "*presume, protect, and defend the ideal of superiority of whites and the inferiority of blacks*" (A. Leon Higginbotham Jr., *Shades of Freedom: Racial Politics and Presumptions of the American Legal System* [New York: Oxford University Press, 1996], xxv). Such claims are dismissed by Bork as "silly."

92. Robert H. Bork, *The Tempting of America: The Political Seduction of the Law* (New York: Free Press, 1990), 342.

93. This quotation by Bork in *The Tempting of America* (342) is taken from the work of his former friend and colleague Alexander Bickel, *The Morality of Consent* (New Haven, Conn.: Yale University Press, 1975), 137, 140.

94. Bork, *Slouching towards Gomorrah*, 246. This account was taken by Bork from Nino Langiulli's essay "When It Came to 'That' at the University of Cincinnati," *Measure* (March 1993): 3.

95. Bork, *Slouching towards Gomorrah*, 247.

96. *New York Times*, April 13, 1996.

97. *New York Times*, April 6, 1998.

98. Ibid.

99. Paul Krugman, "Superiority Complex," *New Republic*, Nov. 3, 1997.

100. Kevin Phillips, *The Politics of Rich and Poor: Wealth and the American Electorate in the Reagan Aftermath* (New York: HarperPerennial, 1991), 18.

101. Ibid., 14.

102. *New York Times*, April 6, 1998.

103. Juliet B. Schor, *The Overspent American: Upscaling, Downshifting, and the New Consumer* (New York: Basic Books, 1998), 18.

104. Andrew P. Morrison, *The Culture of Shame* (New York: Ballantine Books, 1996), 35.

105. Ibid.
106. Schor, *Overspent American,* 3.
107. Ibid., 12–13.
108. Ibid., 55.
109. Ibid., 39.
110. Ibid., 96–97.
111. Harris, "Whiteness as Property," 1715.
112. Schor, *Overspent American,* 28.
113. Ibid., 30.
114. Ibid., 20.
115. Ibid., 21.
116. Ibid., 57.
117. Ibid., 59.
118. Ibid., 160.

## Chapter 6: A Primer

1. My discussion and analysis of a sense of a core self are based on the pioneering work of developmental psychologist Daniel N. Stern in *The Interpersonal World of the Infant: A View from Psychoanalysis and Developmental Psychology* (New York: Basic Books, 1985), 26–27, 69–123. Stern entered developmental psychology because he found the philosophic and psychoanalytic notions associated with classic Freudian theory inadequate to describe the complex worlds of experience he encountered during his residency as he attempted to compile clinical histories of his clients. As Stern notes in the preface to *The Interpersonal World of the Infant,* he found his attempts to give a coherent account of his infant patients' preverbal and preoedipal influences "agonizing." He was forced to "pick and choose" among fragments of recollections by his patients that would "fit" the prevalent theories. This strategy reduced his case studies to an aggravating sameness in the face of people who were quite different. In contrast, Stern found the current research in developmental psychology promising. It could provide him with new approaches and tools for finding out more about the earliest periods of psychological development in the infant. Instead of examining the clinical child — the patient's recollection of her or his childhood — Stern thus turned to direct observation of infants.

Stern also acknowledged his own private attraction to such direct, empirical work with infants and children:

> When I was seven or so, I remember watching an adult try to deal with an infant of one or two years. At that moment it seemed to me so obvious what the infant was all about, but the adult seemed not to understand it at all. It occurred to me that I was at a pivotal age. I knew the infant's "language" but also knew the adult's. I was still "bilingual" and wondered if that facility had to be lost as I grew older.
>
> This early incident has a history of its own. As an infant, I spent considerable time in the hospital, and in order to know what was going on, I became a watcher, a reader of the nonverbal. I never did grow out of it. So

> when halfway through my residency I finally discovered the ethologists, it
> was with great excitement. They offered a scientific approach to the study
> of the naturally occurring nonverbal language of infancy. (ix)

Stern later refers to this noncognitive, interaffective mode of human relationship
as the "dark core" of intersubjectivity.

2. Several books are readily available for more extended discussions of this
experience. My use of the page to describe the relational experience of life is in-
spired by Buddhist monk Thich Nhat Hanh in *The Heart of Understanding:
Commentaries on the Prajnaparamita Heart Sutra,* ed. Peter Levitt (Berkeley,
Calif.: Parallax Press, 1988), who uses a page of his book to describe what he
means by "interbeing." He begins this explanation as follows: "If you are a
poet, you will see clearly that there is a cloud floating in this sheet of paper.
Without a cloud, there will be no rain; without rain, the trees cannot grow;
and without trees, we cannot make paper. . . . So we can say that the cloud and
the paper *inter-are*" (3). Hassidic scholar and social philosopher Martin Buber's
classic text *I and Thou,* trans. Walter Kaufmann (New York: Charles Scribner's
Sons, 1970), is another book that focuses on this relational structure of life. In
the Christian tradition, Friedrich Schleiermacher's *On Religion: Speeches to Its
Cultured Despisers,* trans. Richard Crouter (New York: Cambridge University
Press, 1988), is a classic in the field of modern Protestant theological studies.
*Schleiermacher's Soliloquies,* trans. Horace Leland Friess (Chicago: Open Court,
1957), is also an excellent source for a delineation of the self as always in relationship to its surrounding environment and thus as also an embedded part
and expression of it. The primary Western philosophical text that delineates the
structure of this self-combining "I" is, of course, Immanuel Kant's *Critique of
Pure Reason,* trans. Norman Kemp Smith (New York: Macmillan, 1965). My
book *The Embodied Self: Friedrich Schleiermacher's Solution to Kant's Problem
of the Empirical Self* (Albany: State University of New York Press, 1995) demonstrates how the philosophic and religious notions of the self as a relational
activity converge in the work of Kant and Schleiermacher.

3. Stern, *Interpersonal World,"* 26–27.

4. Ibid.

5. Ibid., 26.

6. Ibid., 125.

7. George Butterworth, "An Ecological Perspective on the Origins of the
Self," in *The Body and the Self* (Cambridge, Mass.: MIT Press, 1998), 101.

8. Heinz Kohut, *How Does Analysis Cure?* ed. Arnold Goldberg with the
collaboration of Paul E. Stepansky (Chicago: University of Chicago Press, 1984),
63, 61, 53. Kohut's use of "I" and "You" to characterize this relationship is akin
to Martin Buber's own understanding of these terms as explained poetically in *I
and Thou* and more philosophically in his edited collection of papers, *On Intersubjectivity and Cultural Creativity,* ed. S. N. Eisenstadt (Chicago: University of
Chicago Press, 1992).

9. Stern, *Interpersonal World,* 27.

10. Martin Buber created the primary word *I-Thou* to refer to our awareness of ourselves as mutually engaged with another person or thing with a

different core of experience. Buber calls our attempt to think of ourselves as an isolated, discrete "I" an "I-It" attitude toward the world.

11. Butterworth, "Ecological Perspective," 101.

12. Ibid., 102–3.

13. Ibid., 104–11.

14. Thandeka, *Embodied Self*, 70.

15. Pediatrician and psychoanalytic theorist D. W. Winnicott's called this place of relationship — the intermediate place of human experiencing — the place where we meaningfully dwell. See his *Playing and Reality* (London: Tavistock/Routledge, 1971).

16. This reference to the "we-go" is taken from the discussion of it by Jean Sanville in her book *The Playground of Psychoanalytic Therapy* (Hillsdale, N.J.: Analytic Press, 1991), 16. Sanville's discussion is based on the work of G. Klein, *Psychoanalytic Theory: An Exploration of Essentials* (New York: International Universities Press, 1976), in which this paradigm is formulated.

17. Stern, *Interpersonal World*, 104–8 and passim.

18. Ibid., 106.

19. D. W. Winnicott, "On 'The Use of an Object,'" in *Psychoanalytic Explorations*, ed. Clare Winnicott, Ray Shepherd, and Madeleine Davis (Cambridge, Mass.: Harvard University Press, 1989), 221.

20. Alice Miller, *Prisoners of Childhood: The Drama of the Gifted Child and the Search for the True Self* (New York: Basic Books, 1981), 7–8 and passim.

21. Ibid., 70.

22. Ibid., 7–8 and passim.

23. Ibid., 8. The infant, in short, can be emotionally and physically abandoned. Or as D. W. Winnicott notes: "When it is said that a baby is dependent, and at the beginning absolutely dependent, and this is really meant, then it follows that what the environment is like has significance because it is a part of the baby" (Winnicott, "The Mother-Infant Experience of Mutuality," in *Psychoanalytic Explorations*, 253).

24. Miller, *Prisoners*, 8.

25. The term *veiled Armageddon* is taken from Americanist Sacvan Bercovitch's analysis of Puritans' attitudes toward their own bodies. See *The Puritan Origins of the American Self* (New Haven: Yale University Press, 1975). He also refers to this battle as the "self civil war."

26. Heinz Kohut, *The Search for the Self: Selected Writings of Heinz Kohut: 1950–1978*, vol. 2, ed. Paul H. Ornstein (New York: International Universities Press, 1978), 655.

27. Andrew P. Morrison, "The Eye Turned Inward: Shame and the Self," in *The Many Faces of Shame*, ed. Donald L. Nathanson (New York: Guilford Press, 1987), 273.

28. Ibid., 276–77.

29. Ken Abraham, *Who Are the Promise Keepers?* (New York: Doubleday, 1997), 15.

30. Bill McCartney with Dave Diles, *From Ashes to Glory* (Nashville: Thomas Nelson, 1995), 81.

31. Special thanks to Claude Barbre, who is assistant director of the Harlem Family Institute and also a training and supervising therapist there, for his discussion with me about this passage from McCartney's work and the insight that such environments obstruct the individuation process of the child. From this perspective, as Barbre noted, "The formation of a white identity is an impediment to individuation."

32. The classic 1950 study of such personal modes of behavior, *The Authoritarian Personality*, by T. W. Adorno, Else Frenkel-Brunswik, Daniel J. Levison, and R. Nevitt Sanford (1950; abridged, New York: W. W. Norton, 1982), analyzes the way in which such personalities become the breeding ground for prejudice. As Frenkel-Brunswik notes in her chapter entitled "Parents, Childhood, Sex, People, and Self as Seen through the Interviews": "Since the values of the parents are outside the child's scope, yet are rigorously imposed upon him, conduct not in conformity with the behavior, or with the behavioral facade, required by the parents has to be rendered ego-alien or 'split-off' from the rest of the personality..., with a resultant lost of integration. Much of the submission to parental authority in the prejudiced subject seems to be induced by impatience on the part of the parents and by the child's fear of displeasing them" (257).

33. See Bill McCartney with David Halbrook, *Sold Out: Becoming Man Enough to Make a Difference* (Nashville: World Publishing, 1997).

34. Ibid., 340–41.

35. Ibid., 149.

36. Ibid., 100.

37. Such feelings, of course, are not unique to McCartney. Our entire American culture, in fact, has been characterized as a "culture of shame" by psychoanalytic shame theorist Andrew P. Morrison, who defines shame as "that feeling of self-castigation which arises when we are convinced that there is something about ourselves that is wrong, inferior, flawed, weak, or dirty" (Morrison, *The Culture of Shame* [New York: Ballantine Books, 1996], 13). We should also note here that psychoanalytic shame theory has become a cutting edge of contemporary psychoanalytic thought about anxious, alienated selves who have been broken by the experience of being in relationship with other human beings. Fifty years ago, Paul Tillich had to talk about anxiety as a theological concern that intersects with psychoanalytic theory. Today, a scholar in religious studies interested in interdisciplinary conversations with psychoanalytic theorists must talk about shame.

The widespread interest in contemporary psychoanalytic shame theory can even be given a birthdate: 1984. As Donald L. Nathanson notes in the introduction to his book *Shame and Pride: Affect, Sex, and the Birth of the Self* (New York: W. W. Norton, 1992), the 1984 symposium on shame organized by him — under the umbrella of the American Psychiatric Association and cosponsored by the American Psychoanalytic Association — was the first meeting in the history of psychiatry or psychoanalysis, either in America or in Europe, to focus on the nature of shame (15). Nathanson suggests that "[t]he enormous interest generated by that meeting has produced a flood of books and articles on shame, making it today more trendy than ignored" (22). He does not exaggerate. A fine summary of the field of shame theory can be found in Robert Karen, "Shame," *Atlantic Monthly* (February 1992).

38. Bill McCartney, "A Call to Unity," in Bill Bright et al., *Seven Promises of a Promise Keeper* (Colorado Springs: Focus on the Family, 1994), 157–58.

39. Ibid., 158.

40. Ibid.

41. Ibid., 163–64.

42. *Promise Keepers Men's Study Bible: New International Version* (Grand Rapids, Mich.: Zondervan, 1997).

43. Dale Schlafer, "Honoring and Praying for Your Pastor," in Bright et al., *Seven Promises*, 137.

44. McCartney with Diles, *From Ashes to Glory*, 10.

45. Much to his credit, McCartney eventually had to acknowledge that he had been "living a lie." During this period of his life, he was an alcoholic, his family life was in shambles; and his top priority was his career rather than God and his family.

46. McCartney with Diles, *From Ashes to Glory*, 292. McCartney's use of Satan to describe the efforts of his detractors has a long history in Christian thought. To make deeper theological sense of McCartney's use of this ploy, we must understand the Protestant tradition in which such references are steeped. The Protestant progenitor of this tendency is Martin Luther, who made Satan the source of any person or circumstance that troubled Luther's conscience. For an excellent one-volume work on the function of conscience in the work of both Luther and John Calvin, the second generation Protestant Reformer, see Randall C. Zachman, *The Assurance of Faith: Conscience in the Theology of Martin Luther and John Calvin* (Minneapolis: Fortress Press, 1993).

47. McCartney with Diles, *From Ashes to Glory*, 165.

48. Tony Evans, "Spiritual Purity," in Bill Bright et al., *Seven Promises*, 75.

49. Ralph Reed, *Active Faith: How Christians Are Changing the Soul of American Politics* (New York: Free Press, 1996), 9.

50. Martin Luther King Jr. believed that economic issues for both black and white Americans were inextricably interwoven with the race issue. King's own theological reflections on human sin thus focused on the exploitive practices of human beings. For him, sin was embedded in the twin and inseparable injustices of race and economics that "exploited both the Negro and the poor whites." From the very beginning, his protest movement took aim against a race-infused economic system of exploitation that trashed most of the people it touched: colored and white. See Martin Luther King Jr., "Pilgrimage to Nonviolence," in *Strength to Love* (New York: Pocket Books, 1993), 167–68.

51. Ibid., 169.

52. McCartney with Diles, *From Ashes to Glory*, 292.

53. Abraham, *Who Are the Promise Keepers?* 141.

54. As Promise Keepers staffer Tony Evans says along those lines with regard to the role of the man in his family, "I'm not suggesting that you *ask* for your role back, I'm urging you to *take it back*." See Evans, "Spiritual Purity," 79.

55. Robert H. Bork, *Slouching towards Gomorrah: Modern Liberalism and the American Decline* (New York: Regan Books, 1996), 281.

56. Ibid., 286.

57. Ibid., 286. A lucid and politically astute analysis of the modern history of this decline of membership in the mainline Protestant churches is found in the important book by James F. Findlay Jr., *Church People in the Struggle: The National Council of Churches and the Black Freedom Movement, 1950–1970* (Oxford: Oxford University Press, 1993). A much less interesting and superficial analysis of this trend is found in the work of Roger Finke and Rodney Stark, *The Churching of America: 1776–1990* (New Brunswick, N.J.: Rutgers University Press, 1992). The latter work, at times, seems to be a gloss on the far more in-depth study of this phenomenon by Martin E. Marty in his book *Pilgrims in Their Own Land: 500 Years of Religion in America* (New York: Penguin Books, 1984).

58. Bork, *Slouching towards Gomorrah*, 286.

59. Ibid., 69–75.

60. Ibid., 64.

61. John Calvin, *Institutes of the Christian Religion*, vol. 20, ed. John T. McNeill, trans. Ford Lewis Battles (Philadelphia: Westminster Press, 1960), 3.7.1–5.

62. The following discussion of Augustine's doctrine of original sin is based on his analysis of the meaning of the Genesis story of Adam and Eve presented in *Saint Augustine on Genesis: Two books on Genesis: "Against the Manichees" and "On the Literal Interpretation of Genesis: An Unfinished Book,"* trans. Roland J. Teske, S.J. (Washington, D.C.: Catholic University of America Press, 1991), and Augustine's *The City of God*, trans. Marcus Dods (New York: Modern Library, 1950).

63. According to Augustine, they knew of their genitals only as that which had been conferred upon them to fulfill the divine command to "[i]ncrease and multiply and replenish the earth" through sexual intercourse. Their genitals were for the purpose of procreation. Lust, passion, and sexual pleasure were not associated with this function (*City of God* 16).

64. Augustine, *City of God*, 14.17; emphasis added.

65. Ibid., 16.18.

66. Peter Brown, *The Body and Society: Men, Women, and Sexual Renunciation in Early Christianity* (New York: Columbia University Press, 1988).

67. As Augustine plumbed the depth of his own feelings of alienation and anxiety, he, of course, discovered his own human feelings of shame and concluded that something must be wrong with him. From this perspective, his *Confessions* can be read as a shame treatise.

68. Brown, *Body and Society*, 416–23, 398–99.

69. Modern liberation theology has attempted to return this critical edge to the received tradition of Catholic thought. A fine example of this theological movement can be found in the work of the founder of liberation theology, Gustavo Gutiérrez. See, for example, Gutiérrez's book *On Job: God-Talk and the Suffering of the Innocent*, trans. Matthew J. O'Connell (Maryknoll, N.Y.: Orbis Books, 1991). For a brief introduction to the overall field (Catholic and Prot-

estant), including its formative context of papal encyclicals, see Deane William Ferm's *Third World Liberation Theologies: An Introductory Survey* (Maryknoll, N.Y.: Orbis Books, 1986). For a discussion of the way in which a feminist liberation theology can be established within an "embodied" affirmation of the self, see my essay "Feminist Theology and the Role of Theory," in *Differing Horizons*, ed. Sheila Greeve Davaney and Rebecca Chopp (Philadelphia: Fortress Press, 1997), 79–98.

70. Brown, *Body and Society,* 416, 399.

71. The various Puritan descriptions of the self mentioned in this paragraph are taken from Sacvan Bercovitch's first chapter, "Puritanism and the Self," in *Puritan Origins.*

72. Richard Baxter, *Christian Directory,* in *Practical Works,* ed. William Orme, 23 vols. (London, 1830), 11.80, 136, 226; 6.422–26. This citation of Baxter's work is taken from Bercovitch, *Puritan Origins,* 17.

73. Bercovitch, *Puritan Origins,* 17–19.

74. Ibid., 18.

75. I am grateful to social ethicist J. Ronald Engel, my colleague at Meadville/Lombard Theological School, for calling my attention to this account by Martha C. Nussbaum in her book *Cultivating Humanity: A Classical Defense of Reform in Liberal Education* (Cambridge, Mass.: Harvard University Press, 1997), 152.

76. Ibid.

77. Ibid., 5.

78. Ibid., 87.

79. Ibid., 95.

80. Ibid., 57

81. Ibid.

82. Ibid., 58–59.

83. Ibid., 61.

84. Brown, *Body and Society,* 19.

85. Richard Sennett, *Flesh and Stone: The Body and the City in Western Civilization* (New York: W. W. Norton, 1994), 47.

86. Brown, *Body and Society,* 11.

87. Nussbaum, *Cultivating Humanity,* 92.

88. Ibid., 6.

89. Sander L. Gilman, *Jewish Self-Hatred: Anti-Semitism and the Hidden Language of the Jews* (Baltimore: Johns Hopkins University Press, 1986), 8–10.

90. Sander L. Gilman, *Freud, Race, and Gender* (Princeton, N.J.: Princeton University Press, 1993), 19.

91. See ibid., 20–21.

92. Ibid., 20.

93. James M. Jones, "Psychological Models of Race: What Have They Been and What Should They Be?" in *Psychological Perspectives on Human Diversity in America,* ed. Jacqueline D. Goodchilds (Washington, D.C.: American Psychological Association, 1991), 15.

94. Jared Diamond, "Race without Color," *Discover* (November 1994): 84.

95. Jones, "Psychological Models," 10.

96. D. W. Winnicott, "Fear of Breakdown," in *Psychoanalytic Explorations,* ed. Clare Winnicott, Ray Shepherd, and Madeleine Davis (Cambridge, Mass.: Harvard University Press, 1989), 87–95.

97. Miller, *Prisoners.*

98. Ibid., 90.

99. Heinz Kohut, *The Restoration of the Self* (New York: International Universities Press, 1977), 122.

100. Miller, *Prisoners,* 69.

101. Cheryl L. Harris, "Whiteness as Property," *Harvard Law Review* 106 (1993): 1710–11.

102. Ibid., 1713.

103. Ibid., 1711.

104. Juliet B. Schor, *The Overspent American: Upscaling, Downshifting, and the New Consumer* (New York: Basic Books, 1998), 96.

105. Ibid., 29–30.

106. Jim Goad, *The Redneck Manifesto: America's Scapegoats: How We Got That Way and Why We're Not Going to Take It Anymore* (New York: Simon and Schuster, 1997), 33. Goad describes this attempted escape from one's own background in an intentionally provocative and offensive manner. He writes: "The redneck reminds [white-collar white liberals] of what they used to be . . . and were lucky enough to escape. It's a deep-rooted ancestral antipathy. In white trash, rich whites see the crude Norse demons they like to think they've 'civilized' out of themselves." I am grateful to David Reich, editor of the Unitarian Universalist *World* magazine, for calling my attention to this book.

107. Ibid., 44.

108. Ibid., 55–56. Goad cites the following sources: Howard Zinn, *A People's History of the United States* (New York: HarperPerennial, 1990), 46; A. Roger Ekirch, *Bound for America: The Transportation of British Convicts to the Colonies* (Oxford: Clarendon Paperbacks, 1987), 58; James G. Leyburn, *The Scotch-Irish: A Social History* (Chapel Hill: University of North Carolina Press, 1962), 176; Gary B. Nash, *Class and Society in Early America* (Inglewood, N.J.: Prentice-Hall, 1970), 82; Richard Hofstadter, *America at 1750: A Social Portrait* (New York: Vintage Books, 1973), 34. Also cited is Michael A. Hoffman II, *They Were White and They Were Slaves: The Untold History of the Enslavement of Whites in Early America,* 4th ed. (Dresden, N.Y.: Wiswell Ruffin House, 1992).

109. Goad, *Redneck Manifesto,* 56. Goad cites Thomas J. Wertenbacker, *The First Americans: 1607–1690* (1927; reprint, Chicago: Quadrangle Books, 1971), 33, and Leyburn, *The Scotch-Irish,* 178.

110. Goad, *Redneck Manifesto,* 57. Goad cites Hoffman, *They Were White,* 90–91.

111. Goad, *Redneck Manifesto,* 64–65. Goad cites Zinn, *A People's History,* 44; and Hoffman, *They Were White,* 89.

112. Goad, *Redneck Manifesto,* 63. Goad cites Robert J. Steinfeld, *The Invention of Free Labor: The Employment Relation in American Law and Culture, 1350–1870* (Chapel Hill: University of North Carolina Press, 1991), 88.

113. Goad, *Redneck Manifesto,* 63.

114. Ibid., 67. See Hoffman, *They Were White*, 11, who cites Thomas Burton, *Parliamentary Diary: 1656–59*, 4:253–74; A. Leon Higginbotham Jr., *In the Matter of Color: Race and the American Legal Process: The Colonial Period* (Oxford: Oxford University Press, 1978), 411. Goad notes that Zinn, in *A People's History*, states that "white indentured servants were often treated as badly as black slaves" (37).

115. Goad, *Redneck Manifesto*, 70.

116. Winthrop D. Jordan, *The White Man's Burden: Historical Origins of Racism in the United States* (London: Oxford University Press, 1974), 63.

117. Ibid.

118. Goad, *Redneck Manifesto*, 59.

119. My use of the term *contempt* in this sentence is based on a discussion of contempt found in Susan Miller, *The Shame Experience* (Hillsdale, N.J.: Analytic Press, 1993), 145.

120. Goad, *Redneck Manifesto*, 28–29.

# INDEX